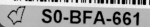
S0-BFA-661

THEMATIC UNIT
Cowboys

Written by Deborah Lybarger and Ruth Fry

Teacher Created Materials, Inc.
6421 Industry Way
Westminster, CA 92683
www.teachercreated.com
©1996 Teacher Created Materials, Inc.
Reprinted, 1999
Made in U.S.A.
ISBN-1-55734-593-7

Illustrated by
Barbara Lorseydi

Edited by
Mary Kaye Taggart

Cover Art by
Agi Palinay

Table of Contents

Introduction

Cowboys is a fascinating whole-language, thematic unit about the adventure and lifestyle of the West, past and present. Its 80 pages are filled with a variety of lessons and activities that are sure to interest and motivate intermediate students. This literature-based thematic unit has two high-quality selections at its core: *Cowboy Eyewitness Book* by David H. Murdoch and Steven Kellogg's *Pecos Bill*. The setting for your students is a trip to a dude ranch where they will explore language arts, math, science, social studies, and art and music in activities that connect across the curriculum. Multicultural and cooperative learning activities are highlighted in this exciting whole-language approach to learning.

This thematic unit includes the following:

❑ **literature selections**—summaries of two children's books with related lessons (complete with reproducible pages) that cross the curriculum

❑ **planning guides**—suggestions for introducing the unit, sequencing the lessons, bulletin boards, and displays

❑ **language arts activities**—daily journal ideas and writing activities to help develop writing skills

❑ **curriculum connections**—activities in math, science, social studies, and art and music to incorporate into your daily curriculum

❑ **culminating activities**—ideas and projects that will enrich the classroom experience and link these new skills to future studies

❑ **unit management suggestions**—teacher aids for organizing this thematic unit

❑ **a bibliography**—suggested readings relating to the Western theme

---

To keep this valuable resource intact so it can be used year after year, you may wish to punch holes in the pages and store them in a three-ring binder.

Introduction *(cont.)*

Why Whole Language?

A whole-language approach involves children in using all modes of communication: reading, writing listening, observing, illustrating, experiencing, and doing. Communication skills are interconnected and integrated into lessons that emphasize the whole of language rather than isolating its parts. The lessons revolve around selected literature. Reading is not taught as a subject separate from writing and spelling, for example. A child reads, writes (spelling appropriately for his/her level), speaks, listens, etc., in response to a literature experience introduced by the teacher. In this way, language skills grow naturally, stimulated by involvement and interest in the topic at hand.

Why Thematic Planning?

One very useful tool for implementing an integrated whole-language program is thematic planning. By choosing a theme with correlative literature selections for a unit of study, a teacher can plan activities throughout the day that lead to a cohesive, in-depth study of the topic. Students will be practicing and applying their skills in meaningful contexts. Consequently, they tend to learn and retain more. Both teachers and students will be freed from a day that is broken into unrelated segments of isolated drill and practice.

Why Cooperative Learning?

Besides academic skills and content, students need to learn social skills. No longer can this area of development be taken for granted. Students must learn to work cooperatively in groups in order to function well in modern society. Group activities should be a regular part of school life, and teachers should consciously include social objectives, as well as academic objectives, in their planning. For example, a group working together to write a report may need to select a leader. The teacher should make clear to the students and monitor the qualities of good leader-follower group interactions just as he/she would state and monitor the academic goals of the project.

Why Journals?

Each day your students should have the opportunity to write in a journal. They may respond to a book, write about a personal experience, or answer a general question of the day posed by the teacher. The cumulative journal provides an excellent means of documenting the writing progress.

Cowboy Eyewitness Book

by David H. Murdoch

Summary

What is a cowboy? Learn all about the lifestyle of these real-life, hardworking frontiersmen in David Murdoch's **Cowboy Eyewitness Book**. *Wonderfully written and strikingly photographed, Murdoch's book takes the reader on an in-depth study of cowboys from the pampas of Argentina to the prairies of the Wild West. It is a great resource and one that your students will pore over during their thematic unit study on cowboys.*

The outline below is a suggested plan for using the various activities that are presented in this unit. You will find these ideas are easy to adapt to your own classroom situation.

Sample Plan

Lesson 1

- Prepare the classroom and do introductory activities. (page 6, "Setting the Stage")
- Read the *Cowboy Eyewitness Book* and discuss the idea of a "visit" to a dude ranch.
- Brainstorm a list of ranch words and do the "Ranch Word Search." (page 8)
- Make saddle bag folders. (page 62)

Lesson 2

- Take pictures of your students for a bulletin board. (page 62)
- Begin writing journal entries. see page 35 and 36 for suggestions.
- Do the "Multicultural Cowboys" crossword puzzle. (page 9)
- Introduce math on the range with the "Chuck Wagon Math" activity. (pages 19 and 20)
- Experiment with "All Directions Point to Fun." (page 50)

Lesson 3

- Solve "Cowboy Cryptograms." (page 55)
- Read and experiment with "Sourdough Cooking." (pages 51 and 52)
- Design and make a bandanna using directions from "Bandanna Art." (page 62)
- Read the clothes section of the *Cowboy Eyewitness Book* and do "Cowboy Clothes Roundup and Puzzle." (pages 14 and 15)
- Form cooperative groups to work on "Baffling Bunkhouse Match." (page 44)

Lesson 4

- Read the section on boots in the *Cowboy Eyewitness Book* and do the activity "These Boots Were Made for More Than Walking!" (page 12)
- Shop for supplies and complete page 21.
- Complete a "Time Line of the West." (page 59)
- Introduce and experiment with "Dressed for Success" and "Fabrications." (pages 16–18)
- Begin the "Cowboy Reports" on page 22.

Lesson 5

- Continue with journal entries. (pages 35 and 36)
- Do the activity, "Nine-Square Puzzle." (page 42)
- Learn multicultural cowboy terms with the "Coin a New Phrase." (pages 10 and 11)
- Continue experiments and observations with "Dressed for Success" and "Fabrications." (pages 16–18)
- Mix up some fun with "Western Cooking." (pages 45 and 46)

Lesson 6

- Play an old cowboy game with "Label It Healthful." (page 13)
- Choose a book with a western theme and write a book report using the activity starting on page 37.
- Introduce chosen culminating activities. (pages 66–69)

Overview of Activities

Setting the Stage

1. Prepare your classroom for a unit on cowboys. Collect books, magazines, and western catalogs to use as reference materials. Bring in cowboy hats, boots, and/or bandannas for the children to wear to really create the feeling of a dude ranch. Hang western posters on the walls and try some of the activities in the art section to give your room a western touch.

2. Ask the students to contribute to the western theme by bringing in western items for a display table. Books, cactus plants, bolo ties, postcards, and western clothing are just a few suggestions.

3. Introduce the dude ranch brochures and the adventure railroad activities on pages 70–74 in the Unit Management section. This will give your students an exciting introduction to the *Cowboys* unit and will also provide an assignment check-off sheet, as well as a brief "Dude Ranch Itinerary" of their trip to the dude ranch.

4. Pack for the trip! Give the students a list of items that they will need to "buy" before they begin their trip out West. Provide lots of catalogs, such as those published by Shepler's Western Wear, L.L. Bean, Eddie Bauer, J.C. Penney, and Cheyenne Outfitters. Use the order form on page 74. Let your students work in cooperative groups.

5. Have students make "saddle bags" for containing their assignments and mementos from the dude ranch trip. Use brown paper bags and the instructions on page 62 to create a great folder.

6. Do not forget the western music! Choose several types of Country Western music that would be appropriate for each activity; a quiet ballad or instrumental for morning work time and more toe-tappin' tunes for art and project times. You might even have a few students who would be willing to teach the class a western line dance.

7. Use the "Morning Starters" on page 75 as a refreshing alternative to the usual before-school work. Each day students can choose their own assignments and cross them out when completed. Many of these could be extended into a "western" language arts lesson.

8. The coupons on page 76 are great motivators and rewards for excellent work. Use them to help promote teamwork, cooperation, and self-esteem.

Enjoying the Book

1. Cowboys on the trail depended on the chuck wagon cook, often nicknamed "Cookie," for hearty meals. Few cowboys would ever think of seriously criticizing the food although it was often the brunt of many a joke. Dish out a meaty assignment with "Chuck Wagon Math" on pages 19 and 20.

Overview of Activities *(cont.)*

Enjoying the Book *(cont.)*

2. A cowboy's clothes and equipment were designed for practical wear and protection. Western fashions today still reflect, in a stylized manner, the garb of the cowboy over one hundred years ago. Have students compare and contrast western wear today with the clothes of yesterday, using a photograph from a book of cowboys. Distribute "Cowboy Clothes Roundup" activities on pages 14 and 15.

3. Who is in charge of the world's time? Discuss why Greenwich, England, is an important place to timekeepers and why it is also important to keep time accurate to the tiniest second. Brainstorm or explain the reason we have leap years. Have students read the "Time Zones and Daylight Savings" information on page 56 and solve the accompanying riddle on page 57.

4. On large ranches cowboys lived in bunkhouses which suited their simple needs for a place to sleep and to hang their saddles out of the rain. The bunkhouse was often the scene of card games, practical jokes, and the telling of tall tales. Divide students into cooperative groups to solve the "Baffling Bunkhouse Match" on page 44.

5. Before handing out compass-making materials, discuss why a magnet is essential in making a compass. Magnets have two distinctly charged ends. Have students experiment with magnets to discover which ends attract and which repel. Discuss the north and south poles of a magnet. Continue with the compass-making project in cooperative groups, using the directions on page 50.

6. Most cattle drives had at least one musician among the cowboys. Although most western movies portray a cowboy playing a guitar by the campfire, the banjo and fiddle were actually the cowboys' favorites. Have teams or the whole class create song sheets for around the campfire. A list of songs from which to choose is provided on page 65.

Extending the Book

1. In preparation for "Dressed for Success" (page 16) and "Fabrications" (pages 17 and 18), have students wear or bring to class denim items (pants, shirts, hats, bags, shoes, ties, dresses, etc.) for a fashion show.

2. Brainstorm modern day uses for a bandanna before or after students create their own "Bandanna Art" on page 62.

3. Devote a corner of the classroom to a "General Store" where students will display items brought from home or designed in class. This can be incorporated into your creative journal writing lessons as well as the math activities in "General Store" on page 21.

4. "Label It Healthful" (page 13) is a great springboard for designing a nutritional bulletin board. Incorporate what we now know about the food pyramid guidelines as you compare and contrast eating habits from the past with those of today.

Ranch Word Search

Listed in the corral are some words related to life on a ranch. Try to find the words in the puzzle below.

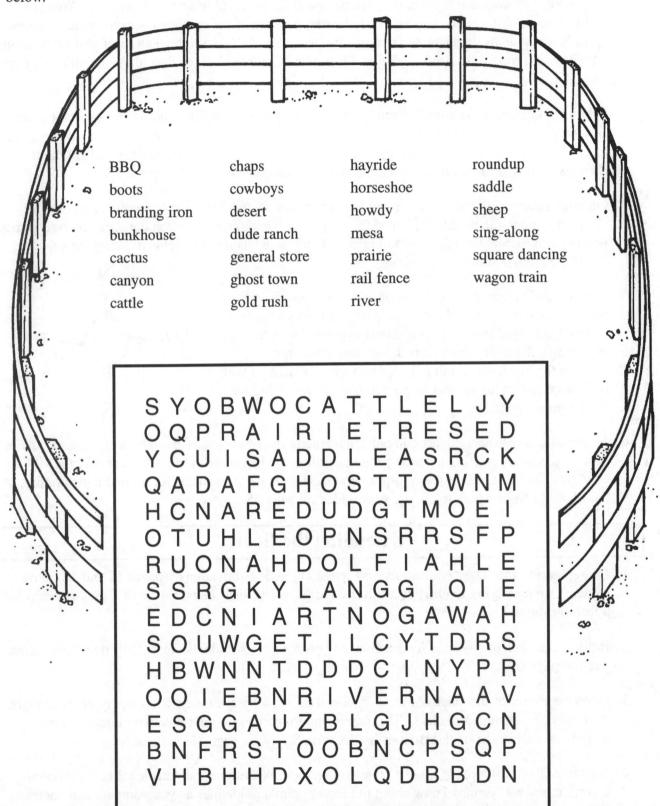

BBQ	chaps	hayride	roundup
boots	cowboys	horseshoe	saddle
branding iron	desert	howdy	sheep
bunkhouse	dude ranch	mesa	sing-along
cactus	general store	prairie	square dancing
canyon	ghost town	rail fence	wagon train
cattle	gold rush	river	

```
S Y O B W O C A T T L E L J Y
O Q P R A I R I E T R E S E D
Y C U I S A D D L E A S R C K
Q A D A F G H O S T T O W N M
H C N A R E D U D G T M O E I
O T U H L E O P N S R R S F P
R U O N A H D O L F I A H L E
S S R G K Y L A N G G I O I E
E D C N I A R T N O G A W A H
S O U W G E T I L C Y T D R S
H B W N N T D D D C I N Y P R
O O I E B N R I V E R N A A V
E S G G A U Z B L G J H G C N
B N F R S T O O B N C P S Q P
V H B H H H D X O L Q D B B D N
```

Multicultural Cowboys

Cowboys are needed all over the world. This puzzle focuses on cowboys from other countries. Use the *Cowboy Eyewitness Book* and other available resources to find the correct answers for the puzzle.

Across

1. Australian ranchers
8. A braided rope
9. Pull tabs on boots
10. A cowboy contest
13. An Australian cowboy hat
14. A Hungarian cowboy
15. An Italian cowboy

Down

2. Leather cover for pants
3. A Mexican cowboy hat
4. A riding crop
5. A Mexican ranch
6. A cowboy from Mexico
7. Cowboys of France
11. A cowboy's seat
12. A South American cowboy

Coin a New Phrase

Often, a new or modern word or phrase has come from another, older word. As you work through this activity, you will discover a word that was added to the English language by mistake.

Directions:

Answer all 10 of the questions, using the words given in the lasso. Write your answer on the next page in the appropriate row of boxes. As you fill in the boxes you will notice that some of the letters in each word are needed to complete the word in the next row of boxes. This is indicated by an arrow pointing to the word below it. If a box has an arrow, simply bring the letter in that box down to the box below it. This will give you a hint about the following word. Once you have answered all the questions, go back and take a look at the answers to numbers one and ten. Through the cowboys' misunderstanding of the answer to the first statement a new word was created which is the answer to the last statement.

1. Spanish cowboys were called _____.

2. Dense growth of bushes or trees is called _____.

3. A term used to define an unbranded critter is _____.

4. A Spanish wide brim hat which was the forerunner of the cowboy hat is a

    _____.

5. A Native American woman who helped Lewis and Clark was _____.

6. A name for wagons in which Western settlers traveled is _____.

7. The people who helped build the transcontinental railroad were the_____.

8. Western expansion forced the _____

    on to reservations.

9. A cowboy's rope is called a _____.

10. The term vaquero was misunderstood. Cowboys thought they were called

    _____.

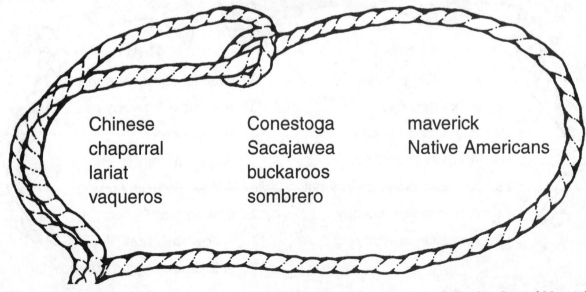

Chinese   Conestoga   maverick
chaparral   Sacajawea   Native Americans
lariat   buckaroos
vaqueros   sombrero

Coin a New Phrase (cont.)

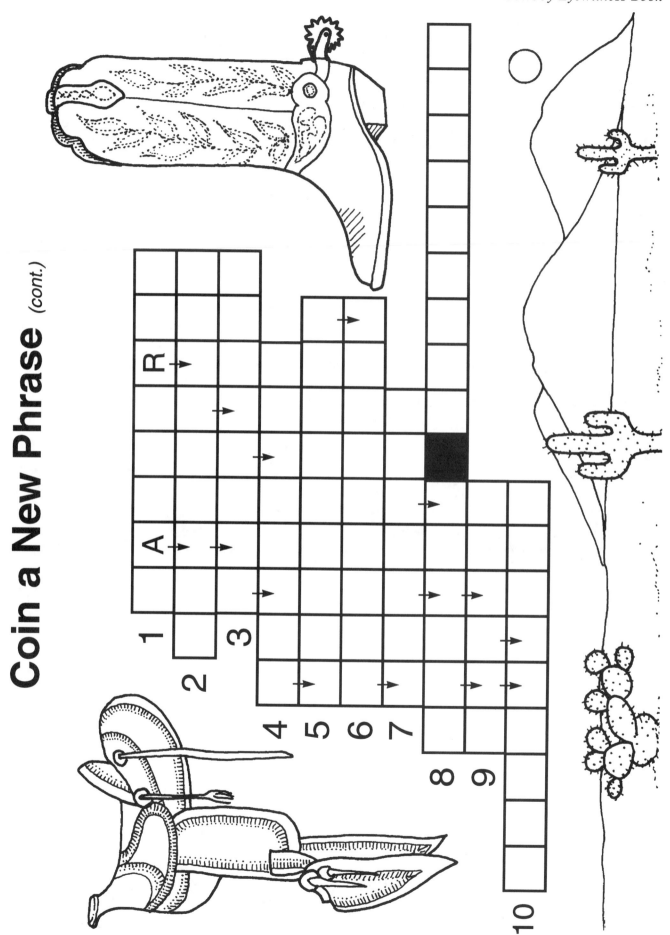

1.   A R →

2.

3.

4.   A → →

5.

6.

7.

8.

9.

10.

These Boots Were Made for More Than Walking!

A cowboy's boots are more than just fashion. Each feature of the boot is specially designed for a purpose to help with job performance and ensure the wearer's safety.

The cowboy boot was first introduced around 1875. The boot maker would make the boots without ever seeing the owner because the order was placed through the mail. The cowboy would send his money, which was equal to about two months' pay, along with a piece of paper with tracings of his feet. About six months later the hardworking cowboy would be wearing his new leather boots.

A boot maker included many special features to meet the demands of the cowboy's rugged life. The 17" height of the boot kept out the dust and gravel that were kicked up by the cattle and horses. This tall stovepipe-like leather was kept stiff around the leg by the decorative stitching. The "mule ears," or loops at the top, were used as handles to pull the boots on the foot. When a cowboy was working on foot, the heel of the boot provided the needed traction so that he could not be dragged by an animal. The heel also kept the foot from sliding through the saddle's stirrup, which was an important feature since it prevented the possibility of being dragged if thrown from the saddle. The sole of the boot was kept fairly thin so the cowboy could feel the stirrup under the foot. The narrow pointed toe allowed the cowboy to slide into the stirrup with speed and ease. The boot's stiff toe could protect a cowboy's toes if they were trampled by an animal.

Today's cowboy boots have changed only slightly from their earliest design. They remain practical and functional.

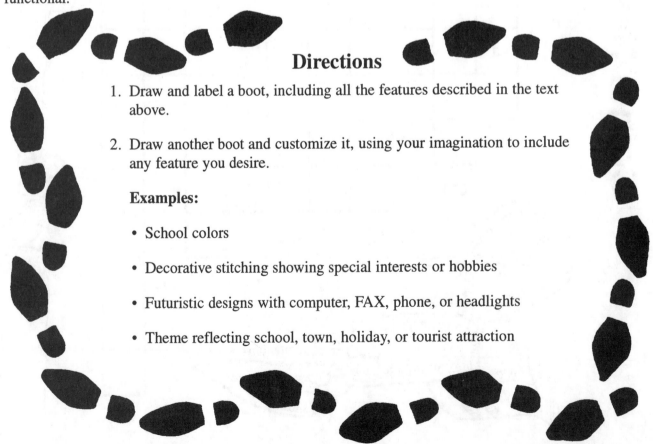

Directions

1. Draw and label a boot, including all the features described in the text above.

2. Draw another boot and customize it, using your imagination to include any feature you desire.

Examples:

• School colors

• Decorative stitching showing special interests or hobbies

• Futuristic designs with computer, FAX, phone, or headlights

• Theme reflecting school, town, holiday, or tourist attraction

12

Label It Healthful

Activities

The early cowboys spent many hours each day hard at work on the ranch, but they also enjoyed having fun. In remote areas of the West ranchers sang, played the banjo or fiddle, and played dominoes. Since books were rarely available, reading as a pastime was unusual for a cowboy or ranch hand, but that does not mean that cowboys did not like to read. As a matter of fact, the cowboys had a reading game that they were able to play without books. Since canned food labels had writing on them and they were accessible to cowboys, games were developed using the information on the cans. A keen memory was helpful when playing one of these games because each person had to study a can label and then answer questions about the details they read.

Design a Food Label

- Create your own canned food label by using a real label as a pattern. Incorporate your own name into your product.
- The federal government requires food companies to include the address of the manufacturer, the net quantity of contents, and the ingredients in descending order. Make sure these are included in your label.
- Options of things to include on your food label include a picture, recipe, coupon, storage recommendations, serving size, expiration date, UPC (universal price code), registered trademark, kosher (complies with Jewish dietary law), nutritional information, and inspection stamps.

Cowboy Memory Game

After everyone has designed a food label, divide into small groups and place your groups' labels in a "hat." Next, as a group, randomly choose one of the labels and study it for a few minutes. Then, hide the label and let the "culinary artist" quiz the group about his/her label. (Example questions: What are the ingredients in the can? How many servings does this can provide?)

A Great Balancing Act

As a group, bring into class one food label from each of the four food groups. Analyze the labels and present your food labels to the class in order from the most nutritious to the least nutritious.

Cowboy Clothes Roundup

Directions: Use the information in the story below to complete the puzzle on page 15.

The first cowboys spent most of their time riding horses, roping, and branding, so their clothes had to be very durable and practical for a variety of needs.

Long ago the hardworking cowboy learned that not just any hat could handle daily wear and tear. The John B. Stetson Company made a good grade, wool felt, ten-gallon hat that was quickly adopted and nick-named "John B." Fashioned after the wide brimmed Mexican sombrero, it served as an umbrella for keeping the sun off the face and for shading the eyes. During the wet seasons, it shielded the face from the rain and helped to keep the rain from dripping down the back of the cowboy's neck. This wide brim was handy for scooping a drink of water from a stream. Also, a cowboy would often fill his hat with grain to feed his horse. During a cattle drive a cowboy would wave his hat in his hand to keep the herd together (this was also known as "hazing"). After a hard day's work out on the range, a cowboy would settle into his bedroll for a few hours of "shut-eye," using his multipurpose hat as a pillow for his head.

Today, it is often considered fashionable for people to wear cowboy boots, but these boots were originally designed to meet the specific needs of the hardworking cowboy. The long, "stovepipe" leg was fashioned after the boots worn by soldiers who spent many hours in their saddles. The decorative stitching on the tall, upper part of the boot was added for support so that the boot would not slide down the leg. These high-topped boots kept stones and pebbles out, and they protected the cowboy from snake bites. At the top of each boot two loops, known as "mule ears," were created for the cowboy to grab hold of while pulling the boot onto his foot. The slim tip of the boot made it easy for the cowboy to slide into the stirrups of a saddle. The high, sharp cut of the heel held the foot securely and comfortably during long hours of riding.

The kerchief, or bandanna, was worn around the neck of the cowboy and was the most versatile part of his wardrobe. A bandanna was often used as a washcloth, a strainer for drinking water, a mask to keep dust out of the mouth and nose, a bandage or a tourniquet for snake bites, first aid, and as a blindfold for a horse when leading it away from fire. On branding day, the fabric became a "piggin' string" for tying calves' legs together.

Leather gloves and cuffs were used to protect the hands and wrists from rope burns. Chaps, leg coverings worn over the cowboy's pants, were worn for protection from thorns and scratchy brush and for warmth in the winter. Spurs on the heels of the cowboy's boots were metal brackets that were used to signal a horse to change direction or move more quickly. Cowboy clothing was often edged in fringe which was originally intended to keep insects away as it moved with the wearer.

The cowboy's clothes were so well designed and so practical that even after one hundred years the costume endures with only a few changes for today's cowboy.

Of all the money that the cowboy spent to outfit himself for his work, the most costly and most important possession purchased was a saddle. A comfortable saddle was a must since the cowboy spent most of his day on the back of a horse.

Cowboy Clothes Roundup *(cont.)*

Directions: Read the clues below carefully. Then, find and circle the answers in the word search puzzle.

Clues:

1. used as a means for directing the horse to do something_____
2. were used as protection for the cowboys' and cowgirls' legs_____
3. a Spanish wide-brimmed hat_____
4. used for protection against rope burns_____
5. when a "piggin string" was used on a calf_____
6. used to strain mud from water for drinking purposes_____
7. protected the wrists from rope burns_____
8. the boot part that helped prevent the foot from sliding through the stirrup_____
9. used to prevent snake bite venom from flowing to the rest of the body_____
10. the nickname for a ten-gallon hat_____
11. loops at the top of boots used for pulling them onto the foot_____
12. what a cowboy would do to keep the cattle together in a group_____
13. a group of cows_____
14. the decorative sewing on the top of the boot_____

J	I	E	L	M	B	H	G	N	I	H	C	T	I	T	S
R	J	O	H	N	B	P	S	S	E	I	N	W	S	T	A
K	I	T	H	C	B	W	E	D	R	E	H	W	R	I	T
T	E	U	Q	I	N	R	U	O	T	U	M	Y	T	H	A
T	A	N	N	A	D	N	A	B	L	F	P	B	R	I	S
Q	S	E	A	L	M	U	L	E	E	A	R	S	I	E	F
G	P	R	E	W	A	N	S	I	T	J	M	I	V	A	F
B	A	E	N	R	S	O	M	B	R	E	R	O	L	O	U
F	H	J	K	O	K	W	I	J	V	M	L	L	R	N	C
Q	C	B	B	R	A	N	D	I	N	G	N	I	Z	A	H
K	D	J	E	M	L	O	K	S	D	P	E	K	V	O	E

Dressed for Success

Levi Strauss, a German immigrant, first sought to make his fortune by supplying tents to the miners during the California Gold Rush of the mid 1800s. The miners' pleas for sturdier clothing to wear while digging prompted Levi to use the material that he had on hand—tent canvas. Using his strong canvas intended for tent making, Strauss created the first pair of jeans. Levi's pants soon earned a reputation for never wearing out. Even the seams resisted tearing. The label proudly represented their ruggedness by depicting two horses trying to pull apart a pair of Levis pants. This remains the company's logo to this day. There are many biographies written about Levi Strauss and his ingenious creation. An enjoyable, fictional account is *Clementine* by Shelley Duvall in her legends and folk tale series.

When canvas was not available, Levi would use the sails of abandoned ships and canvases from covered wagons that made the trip across the country. The fabric he preferred to use to make the popular jeans was imported from Nimes, France. The material was called "serge de Nimes" in French. It became Americanized as denim. Mr. Strauss called his work pants "waist high overalls" because he did not like the common word "jeans." At the time, "jeans" referred to a cheap cotton work pant imported from Genoa, which the French pronounced as "Genes."

Jacob Davis, a Russian immigrant in New York City, developed a method to prevent pant pockets from ripping. He put copper rivets at the corners of each pocket. When he could not afford to patent this idea, he wrote Levi Strauss for help. Mr. Davis and Mr. Strauss jointly filed and obtained a patent for the reinforcements. Mr. Davis then became head tailor at the new Levi Strauss and Company factory in San Francisco, California. The price of a pair of jeans during this time was one dollar.

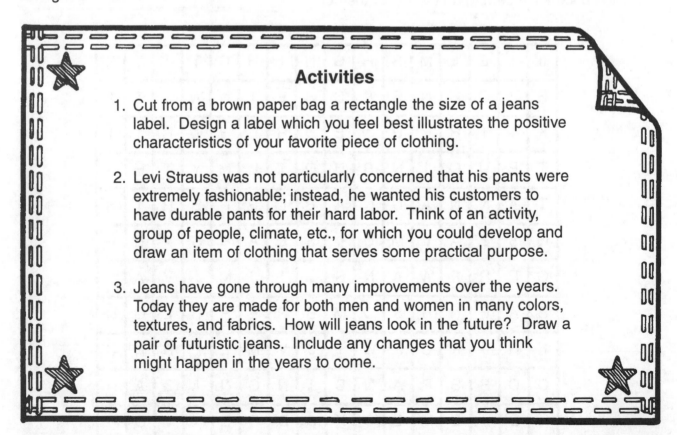

Activities

1. Cut from a brown paper bag a rectangle the size of a jeans label. Design a label which you feel best illustrates the positive characteristics of your favorite piece of clothing.

2. Levi Strauss was not particularly concerned that his pants were extremely fashionable; instead, he wanted his customers to have durable pants for their hard labor. Think of an activity, group of people, climate, etc., for which you could develop and draw an item of clothing that serves some practical purpose.

3. Jeans have gone through many improvements over the years. Today they are made for both men and women in many colors, textures, and fabrics. How will jeans look in the future? Draw a pair of futuristic jeans. Include any changes that you think might happen in the years to come.

Fabrications

Fabrics are designed and produced according to the ways in which they will be used. In this experiment students will determine which fabrics would be best suited for use by a cowboy. Each group will be performing specific tasks to reproduce some of the stress a cowboy would give his clothes.

Organize the class into five groups. Give each group a set of directions (below) for one of the experiments. Before beginning their given experiment, have each group cut old fabric scraps into the size requested under "Materials." As a class, label the five fabrics numbers 1–5 so that they are consistent in every experiment.

	Fabric #1	Fabric #2	Fabric #3	Fabric #4	Fabric #5
Stain Removal					
Durability					
Strength					
Absorbency					
Spur Resistance					

After each team has completed its experiment, the class will gather to share the results.

Reproduce the chart above on the chalkboard. Each group's information will be recorded and discussed. When all information has been given, each student will independently rank the fabrics in order of suitability for ranch life and provide a brief written justification for his or her conclusion.

Team 1

Stain Removal

Materials: 4" (10.2 cm) squares of the five different types of fabrics, detergent, water, "staining" materials, wash tub or large bowl

Directions: Choose three types of stains that a typical cowboy might encounter (examples: dirt, grass, grease, barbecue sauce). Stain each fabric sample with your three chosen stains. Using detergent and water, attempt to remove the stains from each sample. Spend equal time and energy on each piece for consistent scientific results. Let the fabric samples dry. Record stain removal results for each fabric swatch. Rate them, using these three categories: a. easy to remove with no stain remaining, b. moderately difficult to remove with some stain remaining, c. extremely difficult to remove with stain remaining.

Team 2

Durability

Materials: 4" (10.2 cm) fabric squares, medium–coarse sandpaper, stopwatch

Directions: It is the responsibility of your team to hold taut and sand small areas in the centers of the fabric samples, one at a time. One team member should time and record how long it takes to create a hole in each fabric. This is not a race! For accurate and scientific results, your team must try to rub each fabric with the same speed and pressure. Record results based on the ease or difficulty to produce a hole in the fabric (easy, moderate, or difficult).

Fabrications *(cont.)*

Team 3
Strength

Materials: 12" (30.4 cm) squares of fabric samples, scissors, ruler, water, container to hold water

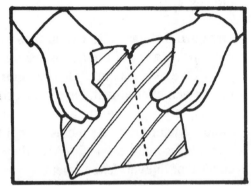

Directions: Make a small cut into each fabric sample 4" (10.2 cm) from a corner. Tear the fabric apart, using your hands, and record whether the task was easy moderate, or difficult. Wet the remaining 8" (20.3 cm) x 12" (30.4 cm) pieces of fabric with water, remove the excess water, and make another cut into the edge of each of the short sides 4" (10.2 cm) from the corner. Tear the fabric pieces apart, using the same amount of energy as before. Record the results again.

Team 4
Absorbency

Materials: water, 1 quart (.95 L) clear glass container, long-handled spoon, 4" (10.2 cm) fabric squares

Directions: For this experiment you will measure the insulation properties of fabric. Fill a quart container nearly full with water. Float one fabric square on the surface of the water and then push it to the bottom with a long-handled spoon. Watch carefully as trapped bubbles of air rush to the surface. The more bubbles there are, the greater the insulation factor of the fabric. Rate the result of each fabric sample as barely, partly, or greatly insulating.

Team 5
Spur Resistance

Materials: 12" (30.4 cm) square fabric samples and a ball-point pen

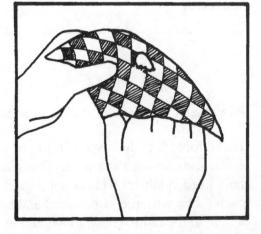

Directions: Using the fabric samples, your research team will be discovering which fabric tears most easily when punctured. Puncture each sample in the center (ask the teacher if she or he will be responsible for this part of the experiment) with a strong ball-point pen. In each fabric sample, place one index finger in the hole and attempt to make the fabric run or tear. Record the results, using the scale of easy, moderate, or difficult.

Chuck Wagon Math

Before the chuck wagon was invented, a cowboy had to carry his food in cloth sacks tied to his saddle or in leather saddle bags slung over the shoulders of his horse. This was cumbersome for the cowboy. Then one ingenious trail rider came up with the idea of a wagon that could carry all the food and supplies needed on a cattle drive. This wagon, designed by Charles Goodnight, still carries his nickname, Chuck. The chuck wagon could travel ahead of the cowboys and the cattle herd, set up, and have dinner ready when the tired, hungry cowboys made camp for the night.

Here is part of an actual supply list from 1885. These supplies would last three months on a cattle drive. Use the list to answer the questions and complete the activities at the bottom of the page.

1885 Chuck Wagon Supply List

10 50-pound sacks of flour	5 50-pound sacks of sugar
5 20-pound bags of coffee beans	5 2-pound tins of tea
2 30-pound sacks of oatmeal	2 40-pound sacks of cornmeal
250-pounds of bacon	4 25-pound bags of beans
2 50-pound crates of apples	3 5-pound boxes of dried prunes
7 25-pound tubs of lard	5 5-pound boxes of raisins
3 50-pound boxes of salt	3 1-pound boxes of allspice
4 5-pound tins of cornstarch	3 10-pound boxes of baking soda
2 8-pound boxes of baking powder	12 30-pound boxes of canned tomatoes*
2 25-pound bags of rice	3 25-pound cases of pickles
4 10-pound jugs of mustard	2 5-pound jars of cinnamon
3 6-pound jars of peppercorns	4 10-pound jugs of pancake syrup
20 jugs of vinegar (1½-pounds each)	

*Canned tomatoes were often a drink to quench the cowboys' thirsts. The acidic snack also counteracted the alkaline dust inhaled by the men on the arid trail.

1. If you were on the trail from May 1 to August 1. How many days would you be away from the ranch?_____

2. On a separate piece of paper, figure the total weight of each supply item. (*example:* 10 sacks of flour x 50 pounds each = 500 pounds)

3. Figure out the total weight that was carried in the chuck wagon by adding up all of the weights of each food item._____

4. It usually took 2 horses to pull each chuck wagon. How much weight was each horse pulling?_____

5. Using the items on the list, make a 3-day menu with 3 meals a day. Try to vary the menu each day to keep those 50 hungry cowboys happy.

Bonus: If there were 50 cowboys on the cattle drive, how many pounds of food did each cowboy consume?

Chuck Wagon Math *(cont.)*

Additional Ideas

You and your class are going on a cattle drive as one of the activities during your stay at the dude ranch. You'll only be gone overnight, but Cookie, the ranch cook, looks like he's packing for a year!

Your dinner menu for the night consists of:

- pork and beans
- hot dogs
- mustard and pickles
- juice
- hot dog rolls

Cookie is sending you to town to buy his cooking supplies. You must figure out how much money you will need so that Cookie can give you enough cash to buy all the supplies for the cookout.

Using a grocery store flier or prices recorded from a local grocery store, determine the cost for each item. You will need to decide approximately how many servings each item contains and how many "cowpokes" are in your class. (And. . . don't forget your trail boss!)

Item Name	Amount Needed	Cost Per Item	Total Amount
pork and beans			
hot dogs			
hot dog rolls			
mustard			
pickles			
juice			
cups			
plates			
spoons			
napkins			
		Total Cost	

General Store

The trail boss has sent you into town to pick up some badly needed supplies. You must buy all the items on the list and have enough money to pay the bill before you leave the store. As you travel through the store to purchase your items, record the price on the line next to your shopping list and deduct that amount from your remaining cash. Remember, you must be able to pay for everything you buy, or you will not be allowed to leave the store. Shop carefully and try to buy things at the lowest prices. Put an X on each square as you create a path through the store. Mark your path with X's; there is no jumping of sections.

3 pounds of cornmeal _____   3 pounds of salt _____   6 dozen eggs _____

5 pounds of sugar _____   5 ounces of cinnamon _____   1 pound of pepper _____

11 jars of honey _____   4 dozen cans of tomatoes __   8 gallons of molasses _____

30 pounds of coffee _____   10 pounds of potatoes _____   6 gallons of vinegar _____

20 pounds of flour _____   12 cakes worth of yeast ____   20 pounds of oatmeal _____

Start with $40.00

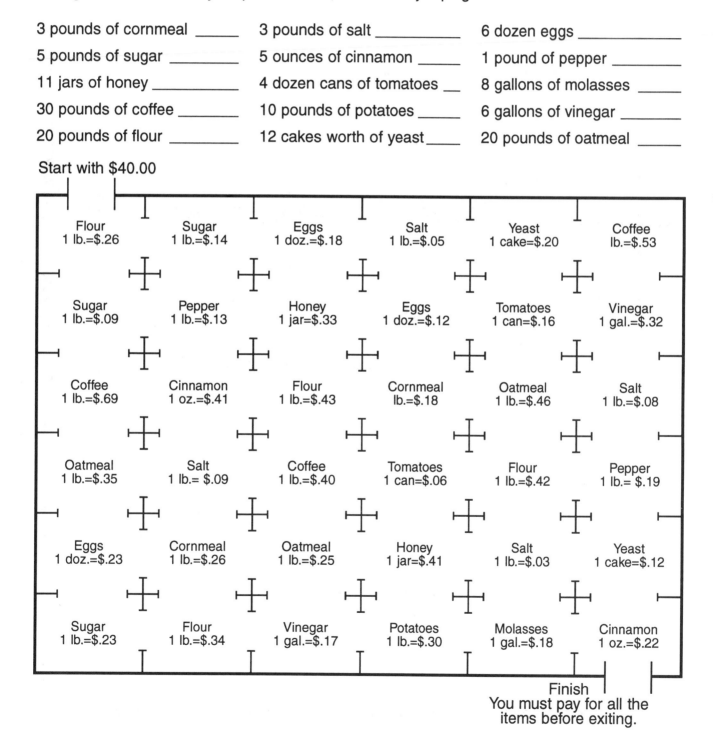

Finish
You must pay for all the items before exiting.

Cowboy Reports

Another activity your class might enjoy is presenting cooperative reports on their cowboy research. Begin by using the *Cowboy Eyewitness Book* by David H. Murdoch as a research source. Divide the class into four cooperative groups. Each group will consist of:

Leader—organizes and directs the group

Librarian—collects research materials

Secretary—records notes for the group

Reporter—reports to the class the group's findings

Group Members—work on individual reports for the project

You may wish to assign each group a type of international cowboy. Each group will be responsible to research and present a report to the class on some of the following areas:

1. **Country of origin**, including a map and flag of the country

2. **Geography** of the country

3. **Cowboy history**, including customs and legends

4. **Vocabulary words**—At least five vocabulary words relating to their specific culture must be taught to the class. This can be done in any creative way the team decides (for example, a song, rap, or chant).

5. **Displays**—These may include costumes, artifacts, stories, literature, videos, filmstrips, artwork, crafts, songs, dances, and/or foods.

22

Pecos Bill

by Steven Kellogg

Summary

The story of **Pecos Bill** *is one of America's favorite tall tales. It is a legend rich in the adventure and heritage of the Old West. The story captures the imagination and lets it grow as big as the frontier the early homesteaders dreamed about. Your students will be captivated by the colorful details and imagery of this story and will be inspired to think and write more descriptively.*

The outline below is a suggested plan for using the various activities in this unit. You will find these ideas fun and easy to adapt to your classroom situation.

Sample Plan

Lesson 1

- Prepare center and do introductory activities in the "Setting the Stage" section. (page 24)
- Discuss tall tales and legends. Read *Pecos Bill* aloud to the class.
- Complete "Pecos Bill Word Search" and "The Story of Pecos Bill." (pages 26 and 27)
- Experiment with "The Weathered Look." (pages 53 and 54)

Lesson 2

- List new vocabulary words from *Pecos Bill.*
- Build "Acrostic Poems" and "Crossword Creations" with the activities on page 28.
- Solve the "Western States Scramble." (page 60)

Lesson 3

- Improve students' writing skills with "Panning for 14-Karat Gold Sentences." (page 29)
- Work in cooperative groups to complete the science activity "Hopin' Your Golden Opportunity Pans Out!" (page 49)
- Extend the western theme with "Grandmother's Quilt." (page 47)
- Read "Time Zones and Daylight Savings" and discover differences in the "Time Zone Riddle" activity. (pages 56 and 57)

Lesson 4

- Use calculators to complete "It All Adds Up to Be Quite a Story." (pages 32 and 33)
- Solve "Stake Your Claim" puzzle. (page 43)
- Discover cowboy humor with "Joke's on You, Dude!" (page 41)
- Introduce culminating activities. (pages 66–69)

Lesson 5

- Complete "The Night Sky and Its Legends" activity and "Star Gazing." (pages 30 and 31)
- Work in cooperative groups to write a legend for a natural phenomenon.
- Solve math problems in "Cowboy Connections." (page 48)
- Practice graphing skills with "Git Along, Little Dogies." (page 58)
- Continue culminating activities.

Lesson 6

- Match the brands in "Your Brand of Fun" activity. (page 34)
- View *Pecos Bill* video by Shelley Duvall.
- Create a time capsule, using the directions on page 61.
- Complete culminating activities.

Overview of Activities

Setting the Stage

1. Create a classroom center for tall tale literature. Have students bring in stories and books that extend the theme. *Clementine* and *Paul Bunyan* are good examples to suggest. Have students draw posters to accompany the books on display.

2. Show the Shelley Duvall video *Pecos Bill* to your students to introduce the theme and spark interest and enthusiasm for reading and writing tall tales of their own.

3. Create some classroom scenery from the story of Pecos Bill. Have students work in cooperative groups to design and paint important scenes from the book. Pinnacle Peak with its four seasons of the year or Pecos Bill's lasso would be good suggestions to get them started.

4. Prepare a bulletin board of students' western-style photographs and autobiographical tall tales of their own creation. Encourage students to dress the part for their pictures. Students can volunteer to read their own stories to the class.

5. Prepare the class to study and record the weather over the course of a week. Use the chart and weather information on pages 53 and 54 from "The Weathered Look" to provide information to get them started.

Enjoying the Book

1. Ask the students what it takes to be a cowboy and live on the frontier. Have a class discussion and list their ideas. Focus on the advantages as well as the hardships of the cowboy lifestyle. Poll the class to see how many of them would want to be cowboys or cowgirls and discuss the changes they would have to make in their lives.

2. Introduce daily writing topics from the "Morning Starters" (page 75) and the "Journal Writing Activities" (page 35). Encourage their creativity by playing soft western music in the background. Have the students keep all their writing samples in their "Saddle Bag Folders" (page 62).

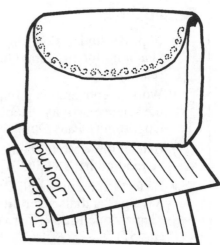

3. After the Civil War, Westward Expansion began in earnest. Many people went west to get rich, escape creditors, evade the law, own land, and gain a sense of freedom. Many freed slaves also went west, seeking new opportunities as free men. Going west also meant giving up the familiar east, leaving loved ones, and facing many hazards in the unknown. Discuss the hardships of travel and the change in lifestyle. Have students attempt to do the "Western States Scramble" (page 60), using their own knowledge before they consult a map. Have them work in groups to share ideas and knowledge they have about some of the states on the map.

24

Overview of Activities *(cont.)*

Enjoying the Book *(cont.)*

4. The 1849 Gold Rush was a powerful lure to many seeking to find great fortune. In your class discussions have the students make a list of things they would do if they struck gold. Both "Panning for 14-Karat Gold Sentences" (page 29) and "Hopin' Your Golden Opportunity Pans Out" (page 49) are great activities to help develop their creativity.

5. In "It All Adds Up to Be Quite a Story" (pages 32 and 33), students will enhance their calculator skills. You may want to work the sample problem with them before allowing the cooperative groups to start.

6. Both written and oral legends are a very important part of our American history. Legends have served to explain many unexplained phenomenons. Extend this lesson into the library where students can research other legends and tall tales. You may also want to suggest some legend journal writing activities to the class.

7. The "Time Capsule Activities" (page 61) give your students an opportunity to think about the past, present, and future. After they complete their cowboy time capsule, you might want to encourage the students to do a personal, family, school, town, or state capsule. Determine the size of the capsule first to limit the items being preserved.

Extending the Book

1. Quilts were practical household items, but they also held many memories because they were made from fabric remnants. Nothing was thrown away on the prairie, and old clothes were fashioned into the detailed patterns we prize today. The "Grandmother's Quilt" (page 47) activity offers a wide range of extension activities. Perhaps there is a grandmother or other relative who would be willing to come into the class to demonstrate quilting and display some of her family treasures.

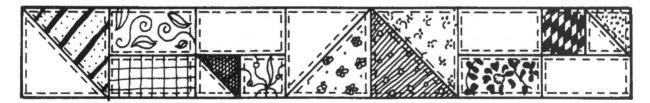

2. Reread the story of *Pecos Bill* and compare it with the video version by Shelley Duvall. The students will find that there are many different versions of the same legends. Place other versions at a center for students to read.

3. "Oregon Trail" is a great computer activity to sharpen your students' critical thinking skills. The graphics are wonderful, and the students will be faced with many challenging decisions as they travel west.

4. A visit to a ranch or farm would be an unforgettable extension of this unit. Try to arrange a field trip where the students can spend the day living the life of a cowboy.

Pecos Bill Word Search

Directions: Find the *Pecos Bill* words from inside the snake in the word search below. Circle the words in the word search.

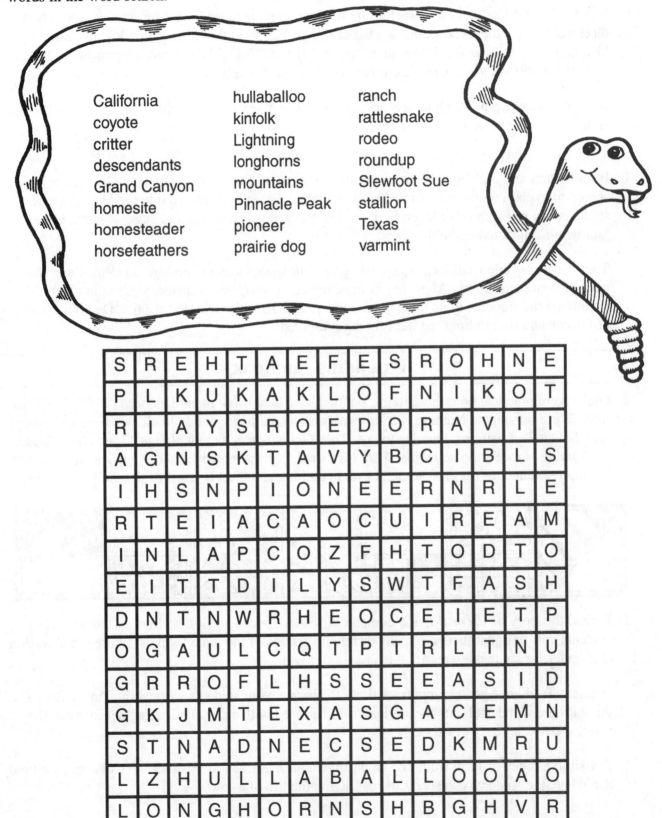

California	hullaballoo	ranch
coyote	kinfolk	rattlesnake
critter	Lightning	rodeo
descendants	longhorns	roundup
Grand Canyon	mountains	Slewfoot Sue
homesite	Pinnacle Peak	stallion
homesteader	pioneer	Texas
horsefeathers	prairie dog	varmint

S	R	E	H	T	A	E	F	E	S	R	O	H	N	E
P	L	K	U	K	A	K	L	O	F	N	I	K	O	T
R	I	A	Y	S	R	O	E	D	O	R	A	V	I	I
A	G	N	S	K	T	A	V	Y	B	C	I	B	L	S
I	H	S	N	P	I	O	N	E	E	R	N	R	L	E
R	T	E	I	A	C	A	O	C	U	I	R	E	A	M
I	N	L	A	P	C	O	Z	F	H	T	O	D	T	O
E	I	T	T	D	I	L	Y	S	W	T	F	A	S	H
D	N	T	N	W	R	H	E	O	C	E	I	E	T	P
O	G	A	U	L	C	Q	T	P	T	R	L	T	N	U
G	R	R	O	F	L	H	S	S	E	E	A	S	I	D
G	K	J	M	T	E	X	A	S	G	A	C	E	M	N
S	T	N	A	D	N	E	C	S	E	D	K	M	R	U
L	Z	H	U	L	L	A	B	A	L	L	O	O	A	O
L	O	N	G	H	O	R	N	S	H	B	G	H	V	R

26

The Story of Pecos Bill

Use the words from the "Pecos Bill Word Search" to fill in the blanks.

Pecos Bill was just a baby when his 1._____

decided to head west. These were the days when many

people, called 2._____s, left the East to

travel to 3._____ or

4._____ in the hopes of building a

5._____ . The family brought all their

belongings as they traveled in search of a new

6._____ . Bill loved to play with all of the

animals, especially the 7._____ . Legend has

it that Pecos Bill fell off the covered wagon as his family was

crossing the Pecos River and was found and raised by a

8._____ pack. One day a drifter found Bill

and asked him what he was doing living with wild

9._____s. When Bill tried to explain that he

was a coyote, the drifter shouted, 10. "_____,

you're a Texan just like me!" The two friends rode west

through the 11._____ until they were

ambushed by a giant 12._____ . Bill tamed

that 13._____ and began to use him as a lasso.

He vowed to 14._____ every

15._____ in Texas. What a

16._____! Some people claim that that was

the first 17._____ . Now all Bill needed was

a horse, and he chased a beautiful 18._____

from the Arctic Circle to the 19._____ .

Finally he caught the stallion and named him

20._____ . Bill settled his ranch on

21._____ , a mountain that was so high it

remained winter at the top all year and changed from autumn

and spring into summer at the base. Bill thought his life was

complete when he met and married 22._____ .

Pecos Bill had become a 23._____ at last,

and his 24._____ still live on his Pinnacle

Peak ranch to this very day.

Word Rodeo

Acrostic Poems

Acrostic is a form of poetry writing which invokes great imagination in children. You may wish to provide students with specially selected western words or, perhaps, let the students choose words from their spelling list.

Examples:

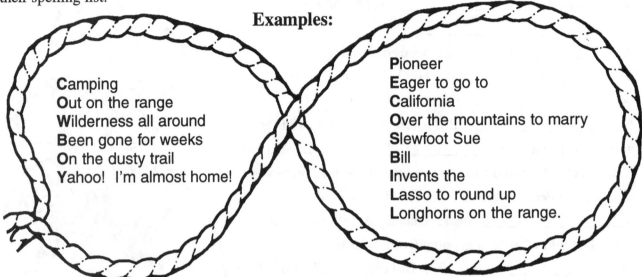

Camping
Out on the range
Wilderness all around
Been gone for weeks
On the dusty trail
Yahoo! I'm almost home!

Pioneer
Eager to go to
California
Over the mountains to marry
Slewfoot Sue
Bill
Invents the
Lasso to round up
Longhorns on the range.

Crossword Creations

Present to your students one word across the paper and have them add other western words of their choosing, in any order, to cross through the original word. How many words can be incorporated into the main word? Another variation on this would be to have the students find words from the literature selection and create a crossword (as in the second example).

Examples:

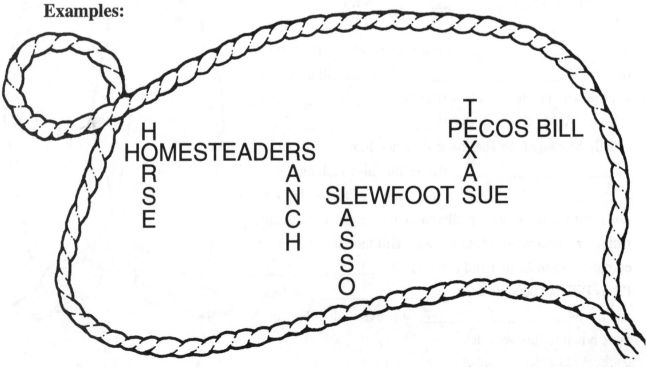

```
        H
HOMESTEADERS              T
        O          R    PECOS BILL
        R          A    X
        S          N    A
        E          C    A
                   H  SLEWFOOT SUE
                      L
                      A
                      S
                      S
                      O
```

Panning for 14-Karat Gold Sentences

A sentence rich with description is more appealing to the reader than an unimaginative, boring group of words. Both will get your point across, but which one would you rather read?

Pecos Bill caught a horse.
– or –
Using a rattlesnake for a lasso, Pecos Bill tamed the wild, bucking stallion.

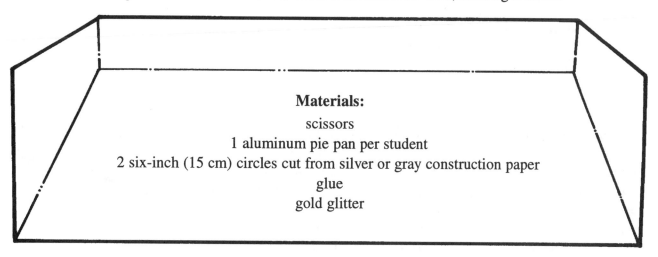

Materials:

scissors
1 aluminum pie pan per student
2 six-inch (15 cm) circles cut from silver or gray construction paper
glue
gold glitter

Directions:

1. Have each student write a short, unembellished sentence.

2. Next, let them transform their simple sentences into dazzling sentences that would grab the reader's attention. A thesaurus may be very helpful.

3. Students will then need to trace and cut out two six-inch (15 cm) circles from gray or silver construction paper.

4. Give them time to write the unembellished sentence in the middle of one circle and then write the new, illuminated sentence on the other circle.

5. Allow students to decorate the dazzling sentence using glue and gold glitter. LET THESE DRY. Then have students glue this circle to the bottom of the pie pan.

6. Finally, the students should make a line of glue on the back side of the short sentence circle at the top only. The short sentence is then to be placed on top of the longer sentence, the glue creating a hinge-like flap.

7. When completed, place all the pans on a bulletin board or in a display case and let the students take turns "panning" for gold by lifting up the plain statements to reveal the sparkling treasures that lie beneath! They're sure to strike it rich!

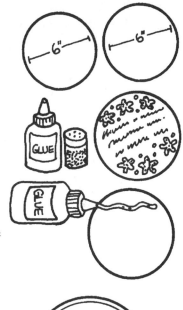

The Night Sky and Its Legends

To relax around the campfire on the open range, cowboys shared stories and legends. On some clear, dark, scary nights cowboys' tales centered around the constellations and the folklore that surrounded them.

The Devil's Tower

In the Black Hills of Wyoming stands an imposing geological formation. For centuries this nearly 1,300-foot tall natural wonder called Devil's Tower played an important role in the legends and folklore of Native Americans. It served as a landmark to the Westward Expansion travelers and is now a popular national monument. You might recognize this stump-shaped column from the movie *Close Encounters of the Third Kind*.

Directions: Read the legend below and complete the assignment that follows.

One day a group of Native Americans were camped by a stream where there were many bears. While playing, seven little girls were chased by bears. Just as the bears were about to catch them, the girls jumped onto a low rock. The girls pleaded with the rock to take pity on them and save their lives. The rock heard the girls' cries and began to push itself up out of the ground. The children were raised higher and higher, out of the reach of the angry bears. The bears scratched the rising rocks with their claws, making deep ruts, but fell to the ground far below. The rock continued to push the children upwards out of harm's way while the bears jumped at them. The seven little girls became immortalized, and you can still see them in the evening sky. Look for the cluster of seven stars that make up Pleiades in the constellation Taurus.

Many other constellations have legends associated with them, too.

1. Research the folklore for some of the other constellations. (examples: The Big Dipper, Orion, or Capricorn)
2. On a 4" x 6" (10 cm x 15 cm) piece of paper, draw the star formation for the constellation you have chosen. Glue this paper to a piece of black construction paper of the same size.
3. Punch a thumb tack through each star in the constellation, leaving holes in the paper.
4. Hold the black paper to the light to observe what your constellation looks like at night.

Additional Ideas:

Design your own constellation and write a short story to explain its origin.

The ancient Greeks had many legends about the stars. Research and compare these stories to the ones the cowboys told.

Star Gazing

Can you round up all of the stars in the sky? Rearrange the letters in each star to form the name of a major star or constellation. Use the list below for help.

Ursa Major	Orion	Betelgeuse
Andromeda	Cassiopeia	Rigel
Sirius	Pegasus	Polaris

1._____

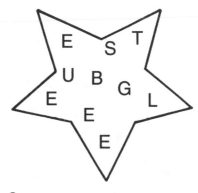

2._____

3._____

4._____

5._____

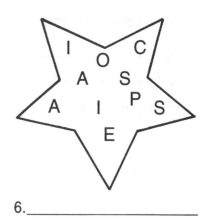

6._____

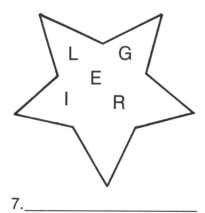

7._____

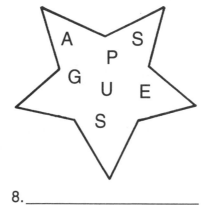

8._____

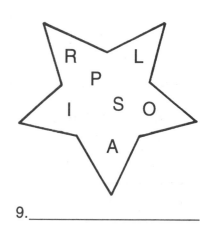

9._____

It All Adds Up to Be Quite a Story

Directions: The answer to each math problem on page 33 will reveal the missing words in the story below. Each digit on your calculator can be read as a letter when turned upside-down. Some digits will be upper case letters while others will be lower case letters.

Example:

$$1.0000$$
$$- .2266$$
$$\overline{0.7734}$$

Now, turn your calculator upside down and see **hELLO!**

There is an old Western legend about a ranch owned by

Pecos (1) _____ and three farmers

named (2) _____ , (3)

_____ , and (4) _____ . They heard about the

Homestead Act passed in the year (5) _____ which promised free land

to anyone who was willing to settle the West. (6) _____ , the three

friends and their wives, (7) _____ , (8) _____ , and

(9) _____ packed their few belongings and headed for Missouri and the

Independence Trail. The small wagon train carried only the bare essentials: food, tools, seeds,

and clothing. The only animals they took were two cows, four (10) _____

and a dozen (11) _____ . The women each packed a reminder of their

lives back East. (12) _____ took a silver (13) _____ that

she had received as a wedding gift. (14) _____ took a

(15) _____ to remind her of the sea, and (16) _____

carefully packed away a delicate, ceramic (17) _____ that was a family

heirloom.

After many months and many hardships the little band of pioneers reached Pinnacle Peak,

Texas. There they built their (18) _____ homes high on a (19)

_____ on land given to them by Pecos Bill, their tough, but generous

(20) _____ .

32

It All Adds Up to Be Quite a Story *(cont.)*

Directions:

1. Solve each math problem in order, using a calculator.

2. After finding the answer, turn the calculator upside-down and read the word displayed.

3. Write the word from the problem in its corresponding blank in the story.

1.   454
     x17
 _____
	2. 439
	     +369
	 _____
		3.
		 $89\overline{)47793}$
			4. 31782
			    − 12
			 _____
				5. 1.962
				   − 0.981
				 _____

6.
 $2\overline{)1}$
	7. 10,000
	   − 4,462
	 _____
		8.
		 $2\overline{)635074}$
			9. 228,716
			   + 83,501
			 _____
				10. 467
				     x 12
				 _____

11.   26,412
   + 8,924
 _____
	12. 2,769
	     x 2
	 _____
		13. 3,869
		    + 3,869
		 _____
			14.
			 $25\overline{)7,938,425}$
				15. 15,469
				     x 5
				 _____

16.   401,479
   − 89,262
 _____
	17. 221
	     x 3
	 _____
		18.
		 $55\overline{)33,385}$
			19. 551
			     x14
			 _____
				20. 3,050
				   + 2,458
				 _____

Create Your Own Calculator Story

Write your own calculator story using the code below to create the math problems.

0 = O	1 = i	2 = z	3 = E	4 = h
5 = s	6 = g	7 = L	8 = B	9 = G

          #593 Thematic Unit—Cowboys

Your Brand of Fun

Cattle are branded as a means of identifying who owns them. When grazing on the open range, cattle from more than one ranch sometimes roam together in search of food and water. One look at the brand tells who owns each cow.

Match the brand symbol with its ranch name. Place brand symbol letters next to the correct numbers.

1. _____

2. _____

3. _____

4. _____

5. _____

6. _____

7. _____

8. _____

9. _____

10. _____

11. _____

12. _____

13. _____

14. _____

15. _____

16. _____

17. _____

18. _____

19. _____

20. _____

A. Arrow J

B. Specs

C. Wind Vane

D. Swing Easy

E. Tumbling A

F. Flying Diamond

G. A Up and A Down

H. Hang High

I. Lucky Seven

J. Hole in Box

K. Whangdoodle

L. Broken Heart

M. Rain Barrel

N. Barbecue

O. Keno

P. OK

Q. Tailed Eight

R. Bow and Arrow

S. Pig Pen

T. Sunrise

Journal Writing

Travelers often keep a written account of their adventures as a way of remembering the details of their trips. They may write about landscapes, people, special sights, foods, weather, transportation, or, perhaps, unusual events. Sometimes they include drawings of sights or an accounting of the money they have spent. You are to keep a journal of the class "visit" to a dude ranch with the following thoughts in mind.

1. "You've Got It Covered"

The first part of this project is for you to make a journal cover of your own design. Strive for creativity! The cover should reflect the theme of travel and/or a ranch, rodeo, or western motif.

2. "Home on the Range"

This is an opportunity for your imagination to roam free. Before you begin to write, visualize a western ranch where you will be spending time with your friends. See the buildings, wildlife, vegetation, geographic features, and other sights in your mind. Now, put your first impressions of this area into words and on paper.

3. "Dawn to Dusk"

Pick a day at the ranch and describe the events that you might experience. This day will begin with rolling out of your bunk at the crack of dawn and continuing straight through until it is time to "hit the hay" at night. You may wish to consult some classroom references to learn more about daily western life.

4. "What a Character!"

This journal entry is a description of your favorite western character. Some possibilities are a real person in history and his or her contributions, a fictional character from the classroom ranch of your creation, or, perhaps, a colorful description of one of your friend's reactions to life at the ranch.

5. "Homeward Bound"

You have completed your vacation at the ranch and are headed home. This final entry in your journal will be one of reflection as you look back on your time spent at the ranch. In what ways have your views of ranch life changed? What did you enjoy most among the activities? In this entry include any misconceptions, new insights, or understandings of life in the West.

6. "Thanks, Folks!"

Now that your stay at the ranch is over, like any good guest following a visit, it is time to take a moment and send your thanks and words of appreciation. As you wait for the train at the station, write a short message on a postcard. Use the postal regulation size of $5\frac{1}{2}$" x $3\frac{1}{2}$" (13 cm x 9 cm) and design a postcard with a western theme on the front. On the back include the name and address of the ranch, a stamp of your own design, and your message.

Journal Writing *(cont.)*

Further Exploration Ideas for the Teacher

Note: The playing of western music during entry writings may help stimulate creativity in the students.

The following suggestions may be used as additional ideas for journal entries.

- You may choose to have your students' first entry be at the time they are "traveling" to the ranch by train through states learned about in an introductory activity.

- While at the ranch a side trip adventure of a wagon train trip to a ghost town may provide for some interesting and creative writings. Students might write about such experiences as eating meals from a chuck wagon and sleeping under the stars.

- The following scenario may stimulate a great deal of creative entries: During a ride back to the ranch at the end of the day, your horse stumbles and you fall to the ground. A sharp pain in your leg tells you that it is probably broken. As you look up, your horse gallops off into the sunset, leaving you alone. You know the way back to the ranch but you're not sure you can walk. In your pocket you have matches, a pocket knife, a dollar bill, and a stick of beef jerky left over from lunch. You are dressed in your cowboy gear. How do you survive until the search party can find you in the morning? What emotions do you feel throughout this ordeal?

- Have students describe a scene at the ranch, using all of the five senses. Challenge your students to make the reader feel as though they, too, can see and experience the place being written about.

In addition to the basic journal assignments, the teacher may wish to introduce the following activity.

Guest Book

In this activity the students create an entry about themselves at the ranch in a guest book. Each student might record:

- his/her western name and its phonetic spelling
- what he/she liked about the ranch
- favorite activities
- favorite foods

You can then collect the information, type the entries, and compile them into a book form for the students. Distribute a copy to each student for a guessing game of "Who's Who on the Ranch."

Guest Book Variations

1. Use famous western characters compiled from the past and present. Have students do research on these people and compile the information in a book of "Who's Who in the West."

2. Use fictitious characters from a working ranch (blacksmith, cook, ranch hand, ranch owners, visiting city slicker, cattle drive boss, domestic help, storyteller, musician, veterinarian, children living at the ranch, gold miner, fence mender, nearby sheriff, etc.) and write a biographical sketch of each person to place in a book of characters. Have students draw a portrait to be placed alongside each entry.

Book Report Ideas

An exciting way to present a book report, while maintaining the western theme, is to have your class make three-dimensional representations of the Conestoga wagons. These wagons were used by the settlers of the western territory and chuck wagons were fashioned after them. Students may choose any book with a western theme, not just those with wagon train settings.

Materials:

- one ½ gallon (1.9 L) size milk carton cut in half lengthwise (creating 2 wagon bases)
- four wagon wheels photocopied from page 40, cut and glued to heavy cardboard or oaktag
- one photocopy of the wagon canvas form on page 39

Directions:

After the students have completed reading their books, have the class complete the following:

1. Prepare a rough draft of a report as described on page 38.
2. Make necessary corrections.
3. Copy the final draft on to page 39.
4. Fill in the character webbing on page 40.
5. Assemble the wagons in the following order:
    - Cover the milk carton half with brown paper.
    - Glue the wagon canvas to the base to make a wagon cover.
    - Attach the wheels with paper fasteners.
    - Add characters and other story related details to the wagon to enhance the project.
6. Make a wagon train display with completed wagons!

Additional Book Report Ideas:

Dictionary of Characters—Make an alphabetical listing of characters, including phonetic spellings, character descriptions, and small, hand-drawn, pictorial representations to put together in a reference booklet. The cover may also be designed by the student.

Mobile—A series of representational shapes determined by the content of the book can be strung and hung in the fashion of a mobile. There are several ways of organizing this project. Each of the major components of a book report (setting, theme, summary, opinion, and main characters) could be given its own shape with text on one side and a picture on the other. The mobiles could also be organized by characters, time periods, or settings.

Book Report Assignment

Recently, we have been on a "field trip" to a dude ranch, and we have seen and heard many stories about cowboys, ranches, and life in the western United States.

Your assignment is to write a book report on a related topic and present it in the three-dimensional form of a Conestoga wagon. Forms and directions to help you build a wagon are on the next pages.

First, choose a book and have it approved by me no later than _____ .

You will use the following directions to write your rough draft. This draft will be where you will first formulate your ideas and make any corrections before you complete the final wagon forms. Be sure you include the following sections in your report.

Setting

This is the time and location where the story takes place, including the town, neighborhood, state, and/or country. The time refers to past, present, or future and the seasonal time of the year.

Theme

In this section you present the message of the story. What lesson do you think the author is trying to get across?

Summary

In the summary section you will discuss the basic ideas of the story. You will summarize the beginning, middle, and ending, making sure to state the problem and how it is resolved.

Opinion

Do you like the book? Write your reaction to the story, plot, characters, and the conclusion. Would you change any part of the story, and if so, what?

Main Characters

List only the main characters of the story. Describe their personalities and their importance to the story.

Use your time wisely. Do not leave the writing of your report to the last minute.

Book Report Assignment *(cont.)*

Glue this edge to the milk carton.

Theme:

Setting:

Author:

Title:

Summary:

Opinion:

Glue this edge to the milk carton.

Book Report Assignment *(cont.)*

Directions: Glue this sheet of paper to a piece of cardboard. Let the glue dry. Cut out the wheels. In the center or hub of each wagon wheel, write the name of one of the characters in your book. Between each of the eight spokes place a word or short phrase that describes the character named in the center.

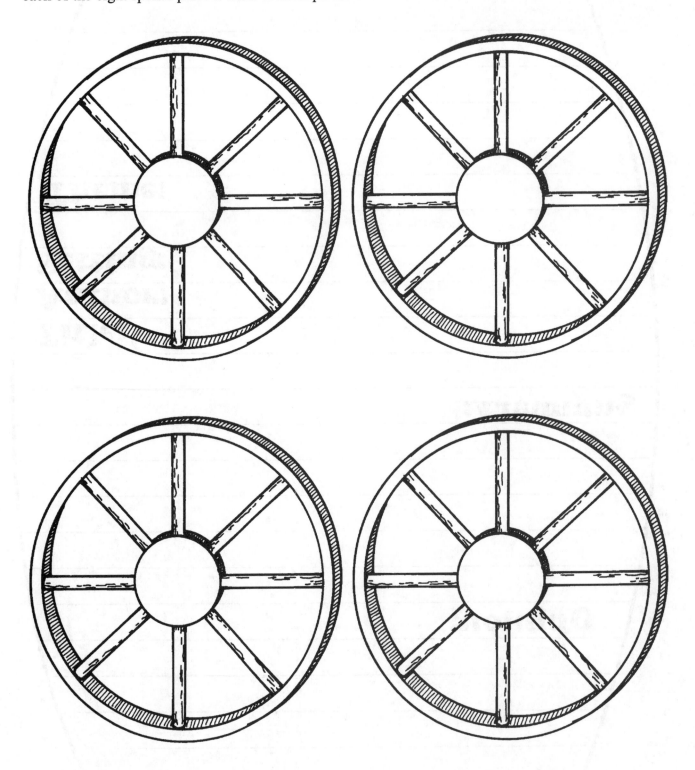

Joke's on You, Dude!

Since cowboys had little money to spend on entertainment, they often played many practical jokes on the new dudes and on each other. These silly pranks were a way to break the monotony of their jobs. Here are some typical jokes:

- Bunks were "short sheeted," and uncomfortable objects were placed in bedrolls for bedtime laughs.

- Another nightime favorite was to send a new dude out on a "snipe hunt" with a burlap bag and a candle in search of fictitious creatures.

- A cowboy who was going "courting" was the focus of many laughs when he would find his horse saddled up and ready to go with the saddle facing the opposite direction. A horse and buggy readied to visit a lady friend might be found rigged with the horse on one side of a fence and the buggy on the other. All this for the sake of a good cowboy laugh!

Joke's on You, Dude!
Test

Now, try this little test on for size and have a good laugh, too! Use the illustration to complete the test.

1. How many brand X brands do you count?

2. The rooster is sitting on the barn roof. If he lays an egg, on which side will it fall?

3. This is a one-story bunkhouse painted all blue. What color are the stairs leading up to the bedroom?

4. Near the bunkhouse is a group of pine trees. In what season do the ranch hands rake the leaves?

5. Circle the "Joke's on You, Dude" test.

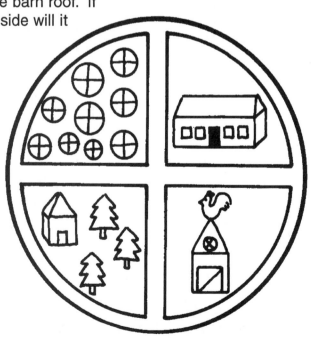

Nine-Square Puzzle

Answer each of the questions below. Then, take the first letter of each answer word and write it in its numbered box in the grid. When the puzzle is completed the letters in order, starting with number 1, will spell something that is important to a person who spends a lot of time outdoors.

Box 4—worn on a cowboy's foot _____

Box 7—a contest of cowboy games _____

Box 1—what a cowboy sits on while riding a horse _____

Box 5—where the cowboy lives and works _____

Box 2—a cowboy gone bad _____

Box 8—a night bird on the range _____

Box 3—country of the first cowboy hat _____

Box 6—a pair of body parts that a hat brim shades from the sun _____

1	2	3
8	9	4
7	6	5

Box 9—Now read what the letters in the boxes 1–8 spell. Draw a picture of this word in box 9.

Stake Your Claim

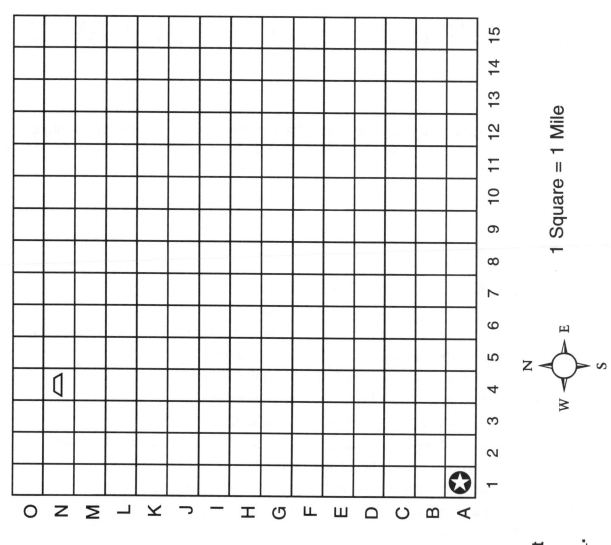

1 Square = 1 Mile

Begin at A1 at the ★

1. Ride 5 miles east and mark a **G** on the square.

2. Ride 7 miles north and mark an **L** on the square.

3. Ride 3 miles west and mark an **S** on the square.

4. Ride 4 miles south and mark an **O** on the square.

5. Ride 9 miles east and mark an **L** on the square.

6. Ride 9 miles north and mark an **F** on the square.

7. Ride 2 miles west and mark a **D** on the square.

8. Ride 4 miles south and mark an **O** on the square.

9. Ride 6 miles west and mark an **O** on the square.

10. Ride 5 miles north. If you landed at the Gold Mine stake your claim! (If not, go back to number one and start over.)

Unscramble the puzzle letters to find what many gold diggers found during the Gold Rush in the West _____.

43

Math

Baffling Bunkhouse Match

Directions: There are five ranch hands, each living in a different-colored bunkhouse, each having a horse, a pet, and a favorite food to eat while on a cattle drive. You must use the clues to match each ranch hand to the correct bunkhouse, horse, pet, and favorite food. Once you have filled in the chart you will be able to answer the questions. The clues are not in order. You must read through them to look for a starting place. Trial and error will get you there. Work as a team, cooperate, and use all of the clues. Good luck and have fun!

1. Beef jerky is the favorite trail food of the person who lives between the green and brown bunkhouses.
2. The black stallion lives between the dapple gray horse and the Appaloosa horse.
3. Trail mix is eaten in the red bunkhouse.
4. The Maverick's prairie dog loves to eat baked beans.
5. The Vaquero lives next to the yellow bunkhouse.
6. The yellow house is between the Vaquero's bunkhouse and the Maverick's bunkhouse.
7. Baked beans are the favorite trail food in the middle bunkhouse.
8. The Buckaroo lives in between the Vaquero and the Maverick.
9. The coyote lives in the house between the prairie dog and the armadillo.
10. The roadrunner lives in the blue bunkhouse next to the rattlesnake.
11. When the owner of the yellow bunkhouse goes on a cattle drive, he eats beef stew.
12. The Vaquero lives in the first bunkhouse on the left.
13. The Cowpoke does not like living right next door to the Cowgirl.
14. It's a good thing the Cowgirl has only one next-door neighbor since she (the Cowgirl) has a rattlesnake as a pet.
15. The brown house is to the immediate right of the blue bunkhouse.
16. The Vaquero's palomino horse is frightened of his next-door neighbor's dapple gray horse.
17. The white stallion in the brown house loves to eat sourdough flapjacks.
18. The Maverick lives in a green bunkhouse.

House Color	Red		Green		Brown
Ranch Hand					
Pet					
Food					
Horse					

Now, answer these baffling bunkhouse questions!

1. Who lives in the red bunkhouse? _____
2. Who likes to eat sourdough flapjacks on the cattle drive? _____
3. Who rides on a black stallion? _____
4. Who has a coyote for a pet? _____
5. Who likes to eat beef jerky? _____

Western Cooking

Effects of High Altitudes on Baking and Bodies

The effects of the high elevations in the western portions of the United States are felt especially by the newcomers to the area. As visitors and new residents experience daily life, they notice marked changes in their food preparation and how they feel.

Problems of baking result because recipes from lower altitudes are usually not satisfactory in high altitudes; the higher the elevation, the more problems there are with the recipes. Recipes need to be adjusted at altitudes beginning at 3,000 feet. There are no definite rules for altitude adjustment because of the great variety of ingredients and amounts in each recipe.

When baking at sea level, a cake will slowly rise and bake until it has a slightly domed top. The same cake recipe baked at an altitude of over 3,000 feet will expand quickly during the baking, break the tiny pockets of air within the cake, and, as the air escapes, the cake will fall in the center. This sunken, high-altitude cake looks as if a fist might have punched it in the middle.

The lower air pressure at high altitudes affects the boiling point of water. Steam forms sooner and water boils at a lower temperature because there is not as much pressure pushing down on the water as there is at sea level. An egg cooked for three minutes at sea level would require about five minutes cooking time at 7,000 feet for the same degree of doneness. The water boils at a lower temperature at high elevations, so the egg is not cooking at the same temperature at each location.

The high altitude takes its toll on the human body, as well as the food being prepared in the kitchen. If you were to move from the low lands at near sea level to the high mountains in the West, your body would have to do some major adjusting to your new environment. For several weeks you may seem very tired throughout the day because your body is hard at work manufacturing more red blood cells. Red blood cells are the carriers of oxygen to your body, an essential part of life. The amount of oxygen in the air at low altitudes is greater than at high altitudes. Fewer oxygen-rich red blood cells are needed at low elevations. Upon moving to high altitudes, the body feels that it is not carrying enough oxygen in the red blood cells, so fatigue begins to set in. Quickly, the body begins to produce more red blood cells to bring the body more of the much needed gas—oxygen. When an athletic event in high altitudes draws contestants from the low lands, often the athletes will arrive several weeks early to train in the higher elevations so the body can adjust to its new surroundings.

Life high in the mountains requires certain skills and adjustments compared to life in the lower elevations.

Western Cooking *(cont.)*

Mix these cooking terms in with the story to cook up quite a tale.

Joe was a bakery chef living on the east coast. When he heard about the California Gold Rush he decided to pursue his dream and move out West. In order to raise enough _____, he took a job as a cook on a ranch. He found the cowboys to be _____ and _____ but he was determined to impress them with his culinary skills and _____ in with the western folks. No matter how hard he tried all his efforts fell _____ . He felt _____ and _____. _____ to the occasion, a _____ cowboy took the city slicker aside and explained about the secrets of high-altitude cooking and the recipe adjustments that must be made. The very idea sounded _____ to Joe, but he _____ through his cookbooks and found the recipe below.

sifted	beaten	dough
rising	crusty	coarse
seasoned	sour	flat
blend	half-baked	

Wild West Two Egg Cake

Sea Level	4000'–5000'	6000'–7000'	10,000'
½ c shortening	½ c shortening	½ c shortening	½ c shortening
1 c sugar	¾ c sugar	¾ c sugar	¾ c sugar
3 tsp baking powder	2½ tsp baking powder	2 tsp baking powder	1½ tsp baking powder
2 eggs	2 eggs	2 eggs	2 eggs
4 c flour	4¼ c flour	4½ c flour	5 c flour
1 tsp vanilla	1 tsp vanilla	1 tsp vanilla	1 tsp vanilla
1 c milk	1 c + 1 T milk	1 c + 2 T milk	1 c + 3 T milk

Joe's cakes have become famous! He needs you to double each of his recipes and put the new recipes on the chart below. This will help him keep up with all his orders as he travels around baking in the various Gold Rush towns!

	4000'-5000'	6000'-7000'	10,000'
shortening			
sugar			
baking powder			
eggs			
flour			
vanilla			
milk			

46

Grandmother's Quilt

Display a patchwork quilt (brought into the classroom by you or a student) in an area where it can be easily seen and measured. Write the following questions on the board or use them to discuss the quilt.

1. What are the outermost measurements of the quilt?
2. What is the area of the quilt?
3. What are the predominant colors of the quilt? Are the colors primary, secondary, or tertiary? Are any of the colors in the quilt complementary?
4. What is the predominant shape used in the quilt?
5. How many quilt squares are in the quilt?
6. What are the measurements of each quilt square?
7. What is the perimeter of each quilt square?
8. Is a border used around the quilt? What is the perimeter of the border?
9. Name all the shapes that are used to make this quilt.

Bonus: Quilt patterns were often given names to describe what they represented. Examples include Ohio Star, Card Trick, Flying Geese, and Morning Star. Bring in books about quilts and ask the students to identify the block names in the example quilt.

Patchwork Quilt Math

Patchwork quilts were among the few belongings that traveled west with the early settlers of the United States. Since fabric was scarce and expensive, the creative women of the West sewed scraps of fabric into quilts that were used as blankets. These practical items were also intricate works of art.

Have each student make a 6" (15 cm) square that will serve as his/her quilt block. Allow students to fill their blocks with geometric patterns of their choice. For example, they may cut out:

2" (5 cm) squares	1" x 6" (2.5 cm x 15 cm) rectangles	6" (15 cm), 3" (7.5 cm),
3" (7.5 cm) squares	2" x 6" (5 cm x 15 cm) rectangles	and 2" (5 cm) squares cut
	3" x 6" (7.5 cm x 15 cm) rectangles	on diagonals to make triangles

Students may use any combination of shapes to fit their blocks.

Additional Ideas:

1. Have the class assemble all of the paper blocks together to make a class quilt as a display on the bulletin board. Or, have students assemble four or six squares of their own as samplers.

3. Using a copier, reduce the students' patterns to use them as note cards.. Each can be colored or painted.

Cowboy Connections

Directions: The dots below represent the numbers 1–100. Solve all of the math problems. Find the dots that represent each answer and connect the dots in order. A few lines have already been drawn for you. When you are finished, you will have drawn a popular cowboy item.

1. $100 - 59 =$
2. $153 \div 3 =$
3. $20 + 20 + 21 =$
4. $500 - 429 =$
5. $41 \times 2 =$
6. $97 - 14 =$
7. $(20 \times 4) + 4 =$
8. $49 + 36 =$
9. $172 \div 2 =$
10. $37 + 50 =$
11. $11 \times 8 =$
12. $200 - 111 =$
13. $4000 \div 50 =$
14. $35 + 35 =$
15. $120 \div 2 =$
16. $50 \times 1 =$
17. $25 + 34 =$
18. $40 + 20 + 9 =$
19. $340 \div 5 =$
20. $25 + 25 + 8 =$
21. $12 \times 4 =$
22. $(3 \times 11) + 5 =$
23. $9 \times 3 =$
24. $10 + 11 + 5 =$
25. $7 \times 5 =$
26. $12 + 12 =$
27. $10 + 10 + 10 + 3 =$
28. $(80 \div 2) + 3 =$
29. $(100 - 50) + 3 =$
30. $9 \times 7 =$
31. $100 - 26 =$
32. $25 \times 3 =$
33. $30 + 40 + 6 =$
34. $385 \div 5 =$
35. $136 - 68 =$

Shape: _____

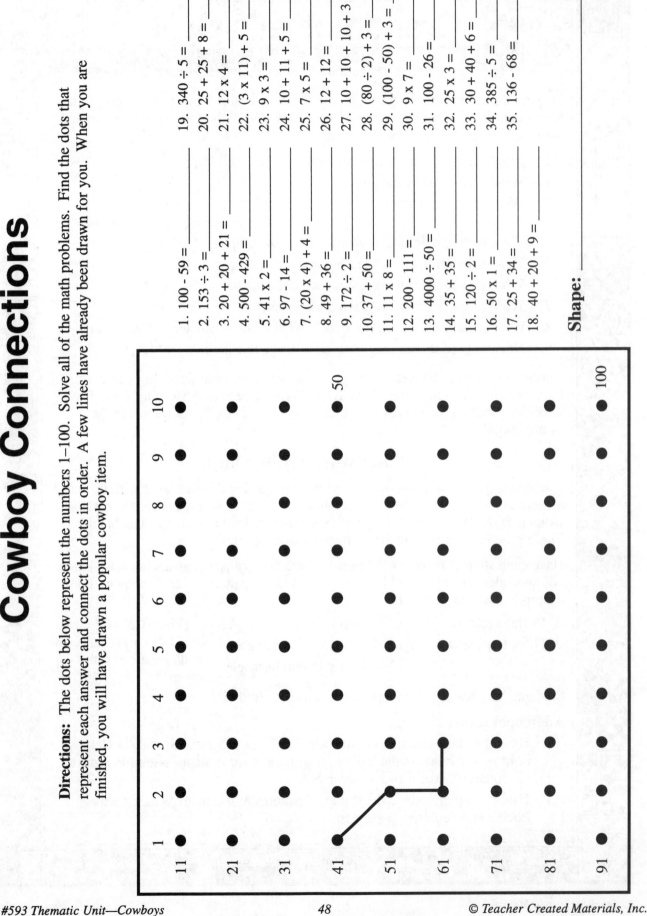

Hopin' Your Golden Opportunity Pans Out!

This is your opportunity to bring a sense of the California Gold Rush to your students in the classroom.

Materials:

- small stones of various sizes or lead sinkers of various sizes flattened with a hammer
- gold spray paint
- scale to weigh the "gold"
- sifter, sand pails, disposable pie pans, shovels (optional items)

Hiding the Gold

You have many options when hiding the gold for the students to discover. The gold may be hidden around the classroom, in a borrowed sand table, outdoors in the school yard, or in the sandbox on the playground.

Finding and Weighing the Gold

The students will locate the hidden gold according to your instructions. Give them a goal weight to aim for. The goal is not to gather as much gold as possible but to gather the golden nuggets needed to match the weight assignment.

To continue this activity use the financial section of a newspaper to locate the current dollar value of gold. Instruct students to convert the weight of their gold into a dollar amount. You may wish to have them create a chart similar to the one below.

Current Gold Value	Weight of Your Discovered Gold	Current Value of Your Gold

Mining for gold was and is still often done by a stream or other water source. The water washes away the silt and rocks, leaving flecks or nuggets of gold at the bottom of the miner's pan because gold is 19.3 times heavier than water.

Science

All Directions Point to Fun

Cowboys were often able to tell directions by the location of the sun and stars in the sky. However, a compass was a handy tool for the cowboy who could afford one.

With a few household items, you can create your own compass.

Materials:

sewing needle	magnet	crayon of any color	tape
cardboard	shallow dish	pen or pencil	water

Procedure:

1. Trace a 1½ inch (3.8 cm) circle on a piece of cardboard and cut it out.

2. On one side of the disk, color heavily to coat the entire surface; this will form a water barrier on the paper.

3. On the reverse side of the cardboard circle, draw a compass rose of your own design, marking the four directions (N, S, E, and W).

4. Rub the point of a needle across a magnet 25 times or more.

5. Tape the magnetized needle to the decorated side of the cardboard circle, making sure that the point of the needle is pointing directly north!

6. Float the disk (crayon side down) in the shallow dish of water.

7. Gently poke and push your compass around the dish and observe that the needle's point will always come back to point north. Why is this so?

Bonus Activity:

How can you tell which direction is N, S, E, or W without a compass? If you are outside at noon on a sunny day, you can do this to find out:

1. Standing outside, look on the ground to see which way your shadow falls. Face that direction. In the northern hemisphere, you will be facing north when facing your shadow at 12:00 noon. In the southern hemisphere, you will be facing south when facing your shadow at 12:00 noon.

2. Raise your right arm up from your side. It will be pointing in the direction of where the sun rises—east.

3. Raise your left arm up from your side. It will be pointing in the direction that the sun sets—west.

Sourdough Cooking

A delicious science experiment for your class is a nineteenth-century staple in western United States cookery, sourdough flapjacks or biscuits! In an era before the manufacturing of commercial yeast, sourdough starter provided the staff of life, bread. It was one of the most important possessions a western cook had. It was something to be well cared for and guarded. The starter was a part of every meal. From it one could not only make bread, biscuits, and flapjacks but also feed the dogs, treat burns, fix a leak between the logs in a cabin, and even repair one's boots. It was the mainstay of the West, and no chuck wagon would leave the home ranch for the roundup without a keg of starter.

When transported, starter was often carried inside bedding so that it would become neither too hot nor too cold. Once camp was set up, flour, salt, and sugar would be mixed with the starter and left to rise near the fire (but not too close or it would get too hot). After it had risen, the dough was put into a Dutch oven (a heavy cast-iron pot with a lid), and then it was buried in the fire's coals to bake.

Sourdough Activities

- Make a sourdough starter in class, using the recipe on page 52. Produce enough for the students to take some home and bake additional recipes with their families.

- Make flapjacks from the starter and have a chuck wagon breakfast at school. Or, use the biscuit recipe on page 52 and enjoy biscuits with your favorite lunch.

To learn more about yeast, try the following activities:

Yeast is made up of microscopic one-celled plants used for the fermentation (the breaking down of molecules) of glucose (a type of sugar) and the production of carbon dioxide for breads. In order to grow, yeast needs a type of sugar such as table sugar, honey, or corn syrup. During fermentation the yeast cells multiply, using the sugar to help them to grow. The by-product of this process, carbon dioxide, allows the dough to rise. Carbon dioxide is what forms the bubbles or the foamy top in the sugar and yeast mixture. It also creates the holes in bread.

A. Growth Properties of Yeast

Materials: 1 package dry yeast, $\frac{1}{4}$ cup (60 mL) warm water, 1 teaspoon (5 mL) sugar, measuring spoons, clear dish or cup that allows for the growth and expansion of the yeast mixture

Procedure: Combine yeast, water, and sugar in dish or cup. Observe the reaction.

B. Making a Yeast-By-Product—Carbon Dioxide

Materials: clear bottle such as a soda bottle with the labels removed, 2 packages of yeast, 1 cup (250 mL) of warm water, 2 tablespoons (30 mL) of water, 1 small balloon

Procedure: Mix the water, yeast, and sugar in the bottle. Place the mouth of the balloon securely over the neck of the bottle. Leave it in a warm place to observe the growth of the yeast and the inflation of the balloon (caused by the release of carbon dioxide gas).

Sourdough Cooking *(cont.)*

▬ Sourdough Starter Recipe ▬

- 1 package active dry yeast
- 2¼ cups (540 mL) lukewarm water
- 2 cups (480 mL) all-purpose flour

Mix the yeast and ¼ cup (60 mL) of the water. Add the rest of the water and flour, stirring with a fork just until blended. Cover the container loosely with a clean cloth, so that the mixture can interact with the yeast that floats in the air. Set the container in a warm spot (70° to 80° F or 21° to 27° C) for 24 hours. The mixture will bubble and have a sour, yeasty smell to it. If it turns orange at any time, discard it. After 24 hours prepare one of the recipes given.

▬ Sourdough Biscuits ▬

Mix the following ingredients in a mixing bowl the day before you intend to bake the biscuits.

- sourdough starter (above)
- 1 cup (240 mL) lukewarm milk
- 1 cup (240 mL) pre-sifted flour

The next day, measure out 1½ cups (360 mL) of the starter mixture. Return the rest to a jar and refrigerate to use later or discard.

Combine the following in a mixing bowl with a fork or pastry cutter until it resembles coarse cornmeal.

- 1½ cups (360 mL) flour
- 3 teaspoons (15 mL) baking powder
- 1½ teaspoons (7.5 mL) baking soda
- 1 teaspoon (5 mL) salt
- 3 tablespoons (45 mL) sugar
- ¼ cup (60 mL) solid vegetable shortening

Add the sourdough starter mixture and stir. Do not over mix as it breaks down the bubbles and causes a heavy dough. On a floured board knead the dough 10–15 times, no more! Roll dough out to ½" (1.3 cm) thickness and cut into desired shapes. Cover and let rise in a warm place for 45 minutes. Bake in a preheated 375° F (191° C) oven for 15–30 minutes, depending on biscuit size. Serve with butter, honey, jelly, or jam if desired. Makes 18 two-inch (5 cm) biscuits.

▬ Sourdough Flapjacks ▬

Mix the following ingredients the day before you want to make flapjacks.

- sourdough starter (above)
- 2 cups (480 mL) lukewarm milk
- 2 cups (480 mL) flour

The next day, measure 2 cups (480 mL) of the starter mixture. Return the rest to a jar and refrigerate to add to later or discard it.

Combine the following ingredients in order:

a. 2 teaspoons (10 mL) baking powder
b. 1½ teaspoons (7.5 mL) baking soda
c. 2 tablespoons (30 mL) vegetable oil
d. 3 teaspoons (15 mL) sugar
e. 2 eggs

Gently mix, taking care not to overmix, which makes for a heavy flapjack. Preheat griddle and grease with a light coating of oil or vegetable spray. Pour 3–4 tablespoons (45–60 mL) of the mixture on the griddle. When bubbles appear on the top (about 3 min.), turn the flapjack and cook it until the other side is brown. Serve with butter and syrup. Makes about 18 flapjacks.

The Weathered Look

In the early days of cattle ranching, cowboys would forecast the weather by observing the subtle changes in their surroundings. Today's ranchers rely mainly on detailed scientific data produced by sophisticated weather instruments.

You will be building a weather station and will be able to record the information gathered from the instruments you have made. Place a thermometer outside to measure the temperature and follow the directions below so that you can measure the daily barometric pressure and rainfall.

Barometer

A barometer measures the rising and lowering pressure of the atmosphere. High pressure indicates clear weather; low pressure indicates less favorable weather.

Materials:

- a clear bottle with a neck (catsup or vinegar bottles work well)
- a clear, narrow glass jar (to hold about 2 cups or 480 mL of water)
- water
- food coloring
- permanent marker

Procedure:

1. Remove all labels from the jar and bottle. Clean thoroughly.
2. Invert the bottle into the jar, making sure the bottle does not touch the bottom of the jar.
3. Fill the jar with enough water to reach just over the mouth of the inverted bottle by an inch (2.5 cm) or so.
4. Add a few drops of food coloring to the water.
5. Release air bubbles from the bottle by tipping it gently.
6. Using a permanent marker, mark the water level on the jar.
7. Place the barometer in a shaded area.
8. Throughout the week, observe the level of the colored water. The water level in the bottle should be high during good weather and low in bad weather.

Rain Gauge

A rain gauge measures the amount of rain that has fallen.

Materials:

- a wide-mouth glass jar
- a permanent marker
- a ruler
- masking tape

Procedure:

1. On a piece of masking tape, use a marker to mark off quarter-inch or centimeter increments. Stick the tape to the jar.
2. Place the jar in an open area away from buildings or trees. Measure and record your results daily. Empty the contents of the jar every day to get accurate readings.

Weather Station Chart

	Monday	Tuesday	Wednesday	Thursday	Friday
Temperature					
Rising or Falling Barometric Pressure					
Rainfall					

54

Cowboy Cryptograms

A cryptogram is a type of word puzzle in which a familiar quote or saying is presented in a secret code. You must decipher the code to discover the message.

Each letter is represented by another letter. You need to crack the code by first discovering the vowels in the smallest words. Then, use these clues to decode larger words. The letters do not follow any specific order and each puzzle is written in a different code. Trial and error is your best method.

Example:

BZNYXSZ AX ARZ UGUZ LWOYR!

_____ ____ _____ _____ _____ !

The decoded message reads:

Welcome to the dude ranch!

In code = decoded

A	= T	Y	= C	L	= R	W	= A	O	= N
X	= O	G	= U	R	= H	S	= M	U	= D
Z	= E	N	= L	B	= W				

The following is a statement made by Will Rogers (1879–1935), an American humorist, actor, and writer who poked fun at great figures of the day in his unique, homespun style. Decode the message in the fashion demonstrated in the example above.

"XAXTZCDVGB VL RWGGZ KL SHGB KL VC VL

" _____ __ _____ __ _____ __ __ __

DKYYXGVGB CH LHPXJHMZ XSLX."

_____ ____ _____ _____."

—Will Rogers
The Illiterate Digest, 1924

Hint: Each code letter V = I.

*Bonus Question: How old was Will Rogers when he died? Show your work on the back of this paper.

The following is the most famous of all western songs and the favorite song of President Franklin Roosevelt. It was inspired by a poem about the West written in 1873 by Dr. Brewster Highley. It was said that Admiral Richard E. Byrd, explorer of the Antarctic, played this song every day at the South Pole until his record player froze; then he sang it.

"SKBQ KP LSQ CZPDQ"

" _____ ___ ____ _____ "

Hint: Each code letter P = N.

Time Zones and Daylight Savings

Why is it that at the time many New Yorkers are enjoying a lunchtime meal, most Californians are eating their breakfast? Why is the United States, as well as the entire globe, divided up into various sections of time?

The divisions of time that surround the earth, known as time zones, clarified some of the problems that once plagued the modernizing world. For hundreds of years each town in the United States decided what the time would be. When the sun was directly overhead, casting no shadows, it was noon. Radios and televisions had not been invented, and telephones were not available yet. Travel was slow by horse and buggy, so it really was not much of a problem that each town was in charge of its own time. In fact, it worked quite well until the railroad was built. Can you imagine how hard it was to print train schedules of arrivals and departures when each town had a different time? This confusing problem was finally resolved in 1883 when the railroad helped devise the system of standard time. Standard time means that everyone in a certain region shares the same established time. Since time zones span great distances, it is no longer necessarily true that the sun will be directly above you at noon. Today, people set their clocks and watches according to the standard time instead of by the sun.

With the new "standard time," the United States was divided into four zones going from east to west—eastern standard time, central standard time, mountain time, and Pacific standard time. Later, when Alaska and Hawaii became part of our country, we added Yukon standard time, Alaska standard time, Bering standard time and Hawaii-Aleutian standard time to the group of time zones in the United States.

In 1884 a conference with countries from all over the globe joined together to develop a system of 24 time zones around the earth. Each segment or zone is 15 longitude degrees apart from the next. It takes the earth one hour to rotate these 15 degrees. Some time zone lines are not perfectly straight because it is often more convenient to follow state or town boundaries. There is an imaginary line in the Pacific Ocean at 180 degrees longitude where all the time zones begin and end. This international dateline is where each new day first begins.

When World War I broke out, a new custom was started in keeping time. During war time resources were scarce. In order to save the coal supplies (which were burned to make electricity), it was decided to move the clocks ahead one hour. This way, there would be more light at the end of the day, and people would not need to turn on their lights as early in the evening. Even after the war ended, daylight savings time continued because people enjoyed having more daylight during the summer months. For a while it was confusing since all the states did not practice daylight savings time. Today, almost every state in our country turns its clocks ahead one hour the first Sunday in April. On the first Sunday in November the clocks are turned back one hour. "Spring ahead—fall back" may be an easier way to remember which way to move the hands on your clocks.

So the next time you sit down to eat your lunch, think about what other meals students may be eating in time zones other than your own. Now that's food for thought!

56

Time Zone Riddle

Directions: Circle the correct answers to each of the statements. Enter that letter in the "Your Choice" box. Once you have all 14 answers, rearrange the letters to discover the answer to the riddle at the end of the puzzle. See the example below. Do not use the answer in the example to solve the puzzle!

	True	False	Your Choice
Example: The automobile industry invented our system of time.	K	S	*S*

	True	False	Your Choice
1. Each state must vote to determine if they are to follow daylight savings time.	M	E	
2. Some of the irregular divisions exist on the map to avoid towns being split into two time zones.	N	P	
3. The continental U.S. has 4 time zones.	D	M	
4. Turn your clock back one hour in the fall when daylight savings is finished for the year.	A	C	
5. Daylight savings time was started during World War II to save fuel.	B	C	
6. There are 20 time zones in the world.	N	U	
7. After World War I ended, daylight savings time continued because people liked having the extra daylight.	I	T	
8. In 1884 representatives gathered to develop a standard system of time.	L	W	
9. It takes the earth one hour to rotate 15 degrees of longitude.	N	S	
10. If you never adjust your clocks to daylight savings time you will be on time for about eight months of the year.	F	R	
11. When the sun is directly overhead, it must be 12:00 noon in all areas of the time zone.	L	D	
12. We turn our clocks ahead one hour in the spring.	H	D	
13. The U.S. government devised the first standardized system of time.	S	N	
14. The grand international dateline is where each new day begins.	E	N	

Unscramble all of the letters that you have collected in the "Your Choice" column and solve the following riddle. Do not include the example letter in the riddle answer.

What are two things a cowboy cannot eat for breakfast?

___ ___ ___ ___ ___ ___   ___ ___ ___   ___ ___ ___ ___ ___ ___

"Git Along, Little Dogies"

On a cattle drive one of a cowboy's greatest fears was the spontaneous scattering of frightened cattle. A stampede could occur at any time because cattle startle easily. A cowboy's riding and roping skills were tested when he chased the cattle back to the herd.

Using this map, help the cowboys gather the stray cattle. Your map is printed with a grid system. The scale in the legend shows that each square represents 1/10 of a mile. Using the compass points, describe the routes used to rejoin the animals to the bull's eye mark in the herd.

Once the cows have been brought back to the bull's eye, total the distance that the cowboys had to travel to round up the wayward creatures. Write your own information on the back of this paper.

Example: The calf hiding behind the chuck wagon would travel **3** squares **south**, **8** squares **west**, and **2** squares **north** to return to the herd.

```
  3 squares south
  8 squares west
+ 2 squares north
_____
13 squares x 1/10 =
13/10 or 1.3 miles
```

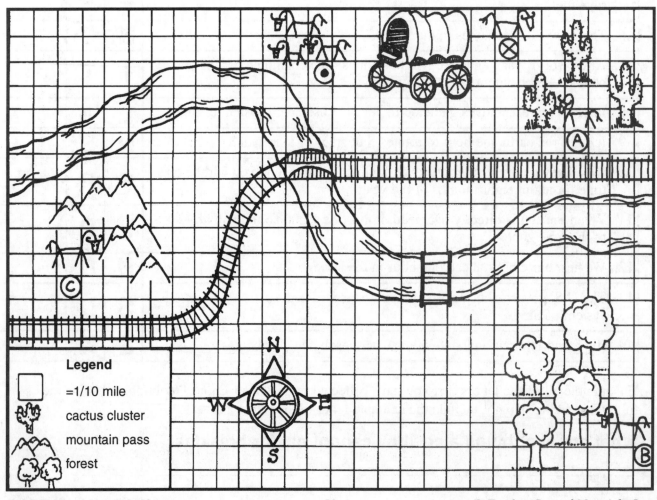

Legend

☐ =1/10 mile

🌵 cactus cluster

⛰ mountain pass

🌳 forest

58

Time Line of the West

Directions: Arrange these dates in chronological order.

```
1860  Pony Express started
1805  Lewis and Clark reached the Pacific Ocean
1862  Homestead Act
1850  California admitted to the Union
1890  Wyoming admitted to the Union
1867  Purchase of Alaska
1848  Gold discovered in California
1876  Colorado admitted to the Union
1869  Transcontinental railroad completed
1889  Montana became a state
1896  Utah joined the United States
1803  Louisiana Purchase
1859  Comstock Lode (gold and silver found in Nevada)
1872  Yellowstone made a national park in Wyoming
1889  Washington became a state
1853  Gadsen Purchase
1861  First telegraph line to California
1869  First Spanish mission in California
1864  Sand Creek massacre
1846  Mexican War began
1898  Annexation of Alaska
1890  Idaho admitted to the Union
1848  Mexican Cession
1859  Oregon admitted to the Union
1876  Battle of the Little Big Horn in Montana
1790  The opening of the Wilderness trail
1804  The beginning of the Lewis and Clark Expedition
1849  Gold Rush in California
1883  Standard time system established by the railroad
```

Beyond Time. . . Bonus Activities

• Choose one time line event and write a brief report. Present it to the class.

• Using a 6" x 36" (15 cm x 91 cm) strip of paper, draw a time line representing the dates above.

• Create a personal time line, marking important events in your life. Use words and/or pictures to represent each date.

• Make a family time line, marking important life events in your family. Ask your family to help you at home.

• With your classmates, recall dates that are significant to the class or school. Holidays, vacations, projects, assemblies, field trips, guest speakers, school fairs, dates of standardized tests, and students' birthdays are a few suggestions.

Western States Scramble

Directions: Below are the outlines of some western states. Cut out, color, and unscramble the states. Glue them on a separate sheet of paper. Label each state, using its full name. Locate and label each state's capital city.

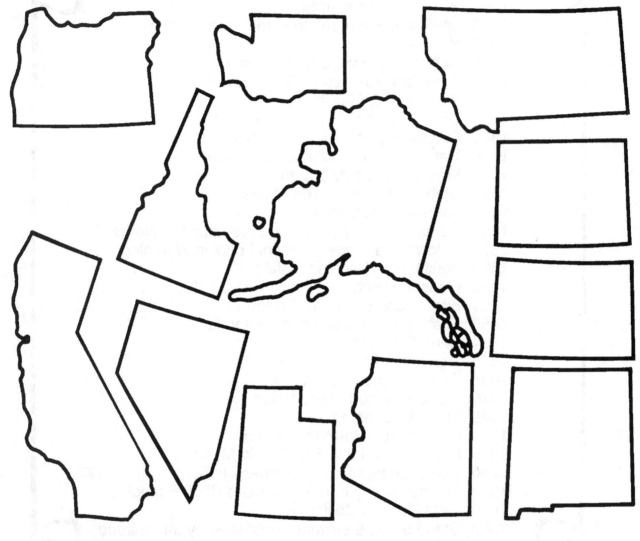

═══ **Bonus Activity** ═══

Choose a state and research the following information and points of interest.

- state bird
- state flag
- state nickname
- population of the state (rank it among the 50 states)
- size of the state (rank it among the 50 states)

- special regional foods
- state flower
- state motto
- natural resources

Choose a geographical tourist site that you would like to visit and describe it.

Time Capsule Activities

=== **Dude Ranch** ===

Imagine you are visiting a dude ranch. During your stay a hundred-year-old time capsule is discovered.

Name ten items that are inside. Describe the function and importance of each item.

=== **Your Turn** ===

Now it is time to assemble objects in a time capsule that will be sealed and opened in another hundred years. What significant items will you place inside to represent life today? List ten items.

=== **Book Report** ===

Present to your class a report on a book that you have read, using a time capsule. The container of the capsule should reflect the book's theme, setting, or characters (for example, lunch pail, cookie tin, sewing box, suitcase, or trunk, to name a few). The items that you put inside can either be real items (newspaper, clothing, gadgets, tools, postcards, letters, photographs) or pictures representing the items.

=== **Modern Machinery in the Old West** ===

Pretend that you could go back in time to the Old West. Write a story about your adventure. While in the past, imagine giving a modern invention (for example, a car, microwave oven, or a television) to an Old West character. Tell how it would change his/her life. What tool(s) would the new-fangled invention replace? How would it have changed history or the lives of the people who lived over a hundred years ago?

Brainstorm your ideas and make a quick list of them. Organize your thoughts and ideas in an orderly fashion and present them in paragraph form. Remember to include an introductory sentence, main body, and conclusion in your work.

Example: power chain saw

A power chain saw would have made the difficult lives of early pioneers much easier. Using ordinary saws for cutting wood usually results in blisters, body aches, and only a fraction of the lumber that can be cut with a chain saw. Clearing land would have been much simpler and faster. The settlers would have had homes that were larger and fancier instead of the simple, rustic, one-room cabins that they built. Firewood would have been much easier to get and stockpile. The chain saw is a great timesaving tool that would have revolutionized building for the early pioneers.

Art Activities

=== **Saddle Bag Directions** ===

This saddle bag is designed to hold the students' assignments throughout the dude ranch visit. The dimensions given are to allow 8½" x 11" (21.5 cm x 28 cm) sheets of paper to fit inside.

Using a brown paper grocery bag, cut two pieces of paper from the inside (to avoid having an advertisement showing on the finished product) or a blank section of the bag. Use the dimensions shown in the first two diagrams below. Decorate the cutouts with a Western theme. Fold where indicated by dotted lines. Place the two pieces on top of each other. With the side and bottom flaps overlapping each other, glue the flaps together.

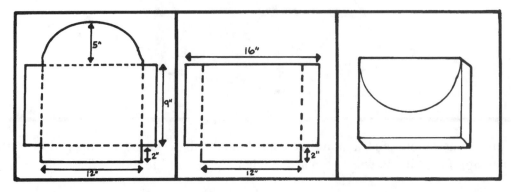

=== **Bandanna Art** ===

Materials: unbleached muslin cloth cut into squares or triangles (make sure they are large enough to tie loosely around a child's neck), fabric crayons, an iron, blotter-type paper for ironing (manila paper)

Directions: Students can use fabric crayons to color their muslin pieces with western symbols and designs of their choice. Instruct them to color their designs heavily with the crayons and encourage them to include their own names (perhaps represented with branding-style letters). When the students are finished coloring, cover the fabric with the manila paper and iron it on a low heat setting. The paper will act as a blotter while the crayon melts into the fabric (use clean sheets of paper for each ironing). Allow it time to cool.

=== **You're Framed, Partner!** ===

Materials: 2 rectangles cut from corrugated cardboard, hats and kerchiefs patterns, paper of choice for hat and kerchief pieces, pencil, scissors, paint, student photographs, glue

Directions: Reproduce the patterns on this page to match the size of the student photographs (school photos work well for this project). Cut one rectangle and glue the photo in the center. Cut a second rectangle with the center cut out. Glue on top of the first rectangle, framing the photograph. Trace, cut, and paint or decorate the hat and bandanna pieces. Glue them on the frame, placing them in a position as if the student were wearing them. Add decorative western touches such as rope edging, western symbols, brands, or painted wagon-wheel macaroni on the front of the frame.

Art Activities *(cont.)*

Win, Place, and Show

Collect and attach ribbons for each completed assignment.

Materials for each student: dude pattern (enlarged to your preferred size), scissors, glue, a piece of cardboard or poster board as large as the pattern, thin ribbons cut to 4" (10 cm) lengths, markers or crayons to decorate with

Directions:

1. Glue the pattern to the cardboard. Let dry and cut out the pattern.
2. Students will decorate to personalize.
3. As assignments are completed in this unit, give ribbons to students to represent their finished work.
4. To affix ribbons to the dude, punch a hole in his chap, fold the ribbon in half, thread the folded end in first, and put the ribbon ends through the loop.
5. On the back side of the dude, students should list the names of the assignments they completed.

Display the dudes on a bulletin board. Make sure that they are accessible so that the students can keep them updated throughout the unit.

Bolo Ties

A bolo tie is part of the traditional western formal dress for men and women. Making one in the classroom is easy and enjoyable!

Materials for each student: cord or plastic lacing, duct tape, a 4" (10 cm) piece of medium weight elastic, a 2"–3" (5 cm–8 cm) cardboard disc (gift-box-weight cardboard works well), paper hole punch, paint, glue, glitter, buttons, puff paint, sequins, stones, seeds, macaroni, foil, yarn, and other decorative items

Directions:

1. Cut the plastic lacing into 40" (1 m) lengths and give three to each student.
2. Braid the entire length, securing the ends with silver duct tape to replicate the traditional silver tips of a bolo tie.
3. Cut a disc from a gift box and punch two, side-by-side holes in the center.
4. Students can decorate their discs with given materials.
5. Thread elastic through cardboard from the front to the back. Tie in a knot to secure.
6. Thread both ends of the plastic lacing through the elastic in the back of the disc.

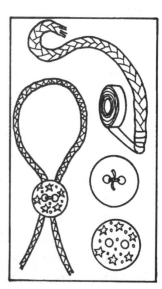

Anna Bandanna and Hanky Horse

As the early settlers of the West rolled across the vast land in their covered wagons, only a few precious luxury items were among their belongings. What was taken on the journey had to be necessary for survival on the new land.

More than a couple of toys for any child was extremely rare in the 1800s. In fact, it was common for a pioneer child to not own even one plaything. Clever children thought of ways to entertain themselves with the ordinary items that surrounded them. Anna Bandanna and Hanky Horse are two characters that were created out of available bandannas and handkerchiefs in the wagon. Childrens' imaginations had a place to grow and flourish with their special friends as they faced a difficult journey to the new land in the West.

Anna Bandanna

Materials:

- 1 bandanna folded in half diagonally
- 1 washable marker
- one of your hands in a clenched fist

Directions:

1. Make a fist and color dots on either side of your middle finger to represent eyes.
2. Tie the folded bandanna around Anna's head with the eyes facing out.
3. Wiggle your thumb on the bottom of the fist to make her talk.

Hanky Horse

Materials:

- 1 square of fabric or a bandanna
- 3 rubber bands
- needle and thread or markers

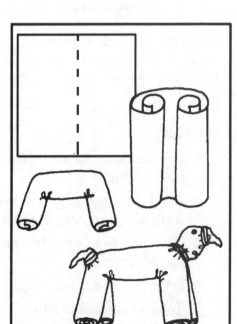

Directions:

1. Fold the fabric square in half, creating a rectangle, and make a crease along the fold.
2. Open the fabric square and lay it flat.
3. Roll the left edge to the center crease. Repeat with the right edge, forming a "log."
4. Bend to form an upside down U shape.
5. At one corner gather and create a small tail. Secure it with a rubber band.
6. At the opposite corner, gather a large bunch of fabric and secure it with a rubber band.
7. Adjust the fabric to form a horse-shaped head and use another rubber band to form a nose.
8. With markers or a needle and thread, add details such as eyes, ears, and a bridle.

     64

"Toe Tappin', Knee Slappin' Music

A day on the trail ended with the gathering and settling of the herd for the night. The wranglers and animals needed time to rest and recuperate after a hard day's work. Throughout the night the cowboys took turns riding around the cattle, singing melodies to sooth the restless dogies. Music was also a way to break the boredom of the quiet nights. Around the campfire, on the range, or at the ranch, music played an important role in the life of all western people. Fortunately, the abundance of western music produced during the heyday of the cowboys has preserved an oral history of the early West. One omission noted in western music is the mention of a wife. Cowboys often fell in love, but their ballads told of heartbreak rather then marital bliss because the typical roaming western cowboy was not the marrying kind.

Even at dances the absence of women was obvious, but that didn't stop the cowboys from having a good time dancing. When there were not enough female dance partners, a cowpoke would tie his bandanna round his arm and pretend he was the lady in the square-dancing duo.

As different ethnic groups settled in the West, each influenced the music. The freed slaves brought the fiddle and the banjo. The old ballads from England and Scotland were the tunes for many songs about the cowboy's lonely life.

You will hear the western influence in many types of American music today; Country Western, pop, show tunes, and classical.

Activities

- Research song titles with a Country Western flair. Compile a list of titles. Read or listen to the lyrics and stories of the pieces of music.

- Display instruments that were popular on the western ranches.

- Play a word game with the letters of the musical scale. Give the students the note names (C,D,E,F,G,A, and B) and challenge them to rearrange the letters into a list of words.

- Form the class into two teams. Have each team take turns writing the notes to melodies of familiar tunes on a musical staff on the chalkboard. At the same time, the other team should try to guess the song titles.

Some suggested song titles for classroom enjoyment during morning work or creative writing experiences follow:

"John Henry"	"Home on the Range"
"She'll Be Comin' 'Round the Mountain"	"I've Been Workin' on the Railroad"
"Polly Wolly Doodle"	"Don't Fence Me In"
"Clementine"	"The Red Pony"
"Billy the Kid"	"Oklahoma"
"Giant"	"Git Along, Little Dogies"

Culminating Activities

As you conclude your visit to the ranch, consider some of the following activities based on a western rodeo theme.

Chuck Wagon Grub

Breakfast

Create a ranch-style breakfast with sourdough pancakes or biscuits and jam. Churn butter in tightly closed jars, using heavy cream and shaking until the butter separates from the watery whey. Other authentic ranch foods might include bacon, sausage, red beans, and canned or dried fruit.

Lunch

Present a ranch-style barbecue complete with wrangler vittles like Rootin' Tootin' Chili, Bronco Baked Beans, Cowboy Corn Bread, and Cowpoke Punch. Serve the meal on aluminum pie plates. Use student-made bandannas for napkins and red and white checked tablecloths. For a quick treat have students cut free-form or cookie-cutter shapes (cactus, horse, cow, sheriff's star, hat, etc.) from store-bought flour tortillas. Toast them plain or with cinnamon sugar or cheese.

Rodeo

Parade

To kick off the grand finale, have participants parade into your rodeo with a representation of the "Best of the West." Have students dress in western garb, carrying colorful flags to a lively western tune. Allow students to create a precision drill as their lines snake about and intersect, forming patterns. You will want to have a video crew (camera person and director) record the festivities.

Games

Continue the celebration with some or all of the following games.

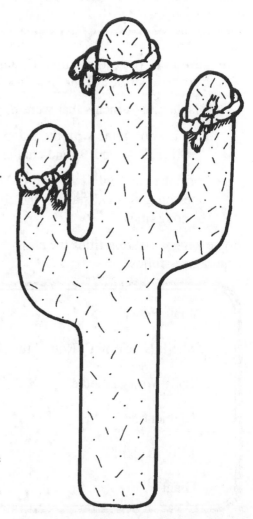

- Bronco Races—commonly known as three-legged races

- Cactus Ring Toss
  Create two or three cacti of varying sizes from pieces of corrugated cardboard. Design them so that they are freestanding. Decorate. Make rings to toss over the cacti limbs from cardboard, rope, or other appropriate materials. Each limb of the cacti may be assigned varying point values according to difficulty. Play according to ring toss rules or modify to suit the needs of the class.

- Roping the Bucking Bronco Chair
  Turn chairs upside down so that the legs are up in the air. Have a roping contest.

Photo Opportunity

- Create a cardboard backdrop illustrating a western scene and snap pictures of students visiting the area.

- Create western characters on a large piece of cardboard. Cut out the faces so that students can peek through for another photo opportunity.

Dancing

Students will enjoy some western-style line dancing and square dancing with lively music.

Culminating Activities *(cont.)*

Make It a Media Event

Magazine or Newspaper

Develop a newspaper or magazine for your classroom ranch. Include the components of a newspaper to reflect the exciting events that have taken place in your room.

Television

With a video camera and other necessary equipment, have a group of students assume the roles of a visiting news crew (camera person, director, reporter, advertising supervisor, and others to suit your production needs). Report on the activities that have taken place on the ranch through food demonstrations, weather reports, agricultural reports, dancing lessons, advertisements, and other topics.

Radio

Create a radio show featuring storytelling (complete with sound effects), poetry readings, music, and interviews.

Classroom Museum

Divide students into groups and assign a different museum display to each group. Label the display items and give tours to groups of younger students.

Bumper Stickers

Cut white contact paper into strips. Using permanent markers, students can design bumper stickers for the ranch or rodeo. These would make a festive bulletin board.

Silent Visitor

A visitor that would have great impact on your group would be one that your class creates. Using western style clothing contributed by the class, build a dude. Into the arms and legs of the clothes stuff newspaper, molding the body into shape. Create a head and face out of papier-mâché, an inverted polystyrene gallon milk container, balloon, or a lady's stuffed stocking. Paint a face. Add yarn or raffia for hair and cover the head with a bandanna and a hat. Students can add and change details by giving him and/or her a guitar, fiddle, harmonica, bridle and saddle, bale of hay to sit on, or perhaps just a can of beans! As your class visitor is being created, be sure to discuss the functional aspect of the western clothing.

Gather 'Round the Campfire

Gather the students around a classroom campfire made from cardboard tubes, yellow and orange cellophane, and flashlights. Turn off the overhead classroom lights. Share ghost stories, stories of long-ago cattle drives, cowboy poems, and sing lots of favorite campfire songs ("Home on the Range," "Clementine," "Sweet Betsy From Pike," "Oh, Susanna," "I've Been Workin' on the Railroad," "Red River Valley," "Down by the Station," "Skip to My Lou," "I've Got Spurs That Jingle, Jangle, Jingle").

Spur of the Moment

Game Directions

Materials:

- pencils and paper
- game sheets

Directions:

- The game may be played in as many rounds as desired.
- Give each student a game sheet. Before the game begins, the teacher establishes the letter to be used for game one, and the students will write it in the space provided on the game sheet.
- Students are to think of a word in each category that begins with the given letter and then write the word on the category blank. There are often blank spaces left at the end of the game.
- When the teacher calls "Time," students are to put their pens or pencils down and begin the scoring.

Scoring:

In turn, the students may read their answers aloud.

- All acceptable answers are worth one point.
- An answer that is correct and is not the same as anyone else's in the class is worth five points.
- The majority rules when an answer is challenged (take a "thumbs up" and "thumbs down" vote).

After all six rounds on the game sheet are completed, you may want to offer the following breakdown of scores to the class.

> 120–150 = Brainy Buckaroo
> 91–120 = Yeehaw! You're good.
> 61–90 = You're an able dude.
> 31–60 = You're a cowpoke.
> 0–30 = You bit the dust!

Six rounds equal one complete game. The highest possible score would be 150 points (30 answers x 5 points).

Spur of the Moment *(cont.)*

Facts of Five Game

I. Category   **Letter**

  1. something a cowboy might carry in his saddle bag

  2. things at a rodeo

  3. weather terms

  4. TV cowboys

  5. jobs on the ranch

II. Category   **Letter**

  1. western states

  2. names for horses

  3. camp gear

  4. cowgirls' names

  5. utensils found on a chuck wagon

III. Category   **Letter**

  1. cowboy slang

  2. things that would make a cowboy smile

  3. wild animals

  4. tools on a ranch

  5. events at a rodeo

IV. Category   **Letter**

  1. animals at a rodeo

  2. articles of cowboy clothing

  3. things one might see from horseback

  4. names for ranches

  5. food cooked over a campfire

V. Category   **Letter**

  1. cowboy song titles

  2. ranch sounds

  3. folk tales

  4. something found in a ghost town

  5. cowboy movie titles

VI. Category   **Letter**

  1. western geographic terms

  2. occupations of the Old West

  3. constellations

  4. famous cowboys

  5. country western singers

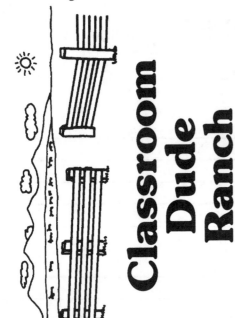

Classroom Dude Ranch

You may begin as a city slicker, but you'll be a weathered western dude at the end of your classroom adventure!

The Best in the West!

Classroom Dude Ranch
Western Town, USA

You've been selected!

It's Your **BRAND** of Fun!

"Yipee Yi-O, it's the best I know!"
—Silver Spur Sam

"Wow! It was a breath of fresh air in our classroom!"
—City Slicker Cynthia

"Hey, dudes, it was a really cool thing to do in school!"
—Lucky Lariat Lenny

70

DUDE RANCH ITINERARY

Assignments and Due Dates

Assignment	Date

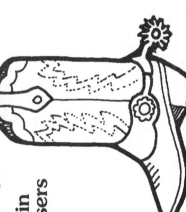

With heaps of fun and chores to be done, your dude ranch field trip has begun!

Featuring . . . .

- Wild West facts and fiction

- Singing around the campfire

- Cooking on the range

- Environmental dilemmas in the West

- Videos, dancing, and games

- Folk tales and legends

- Diary time and postcard writing

- Brain teasers

Howdy Partners,

Saddle up, dudes! Whether you are a greenhorn or ride tall in the saddle, you are sure to realize your cowboy dream as you experience the true West set in the heart of your classroom.

For the first time in its history, your class will be traveling to a dude ranch and participating in a variety of western activities.

So, grab your ten-gallon hats and get ready to live the life of a cowboy for several days.

Happy Trails, Buckaroos!

Your Trail Boss

Adventure Railroad

Directions: Complete the following activity as a class or in your group. Choose a western dude ranch destination by drawing a train route from an eastern city to a western city. Make it a real adventure by passing through several cities along the way. Use dashed lines to show the route (see legend). When your train route is completed, answer the questions on a separate piece of paper.

Questions

1. Name your state of origin.
2. Name the states your train will be traveling through to get to your destination.
3. If each city along your train route represents a stop, how many stops must the train in which you are traveling make?
4. On the map above, what distance will your train travel in inches (cm)?
5. Using the legend on the map above and your answer to #4, compute the mileage to your destination.
6. At a cost of $8.75 per mile, how much will your trip cost?
7. If the train were traveling at an average speed of 65 miles per hour how long would your trip take?
8. Name a city in each state through which your train passes as you travel to the dude ranch.

Bonus: Name a tourist attraction in any of the states through which your train passes.

Adventure Railroad Luncheon Menu

Sandwiches

tuna fish	$2.95
chicken salad	2.95
hamburger	3.25
peanut butter and jelly	1.95

Beverages

milk	$.55
juice	.55
coffee	.65
tea	.65
soda pop	.75

Side Dishes

French fries	$1.95
onion rings	2.50
tossed salad	1.10
coleslaw	.95

Desserts

pie	$2.50
cake	2.50
pudding	1.35
ice cream	1.15
fresh fruit	.75

Adventure Railroad Luncheon Bill

Item	Price
Total	

Please list your choices and their prices on the bill. Kindly show the total cost of the meal at the bottom of the bill. Thank you.

Passenger Ticket
Adventure Railroad

Name _____ Age _____

Address_____

City _____ State _____ Zip _____

School _____ Teacher _____

Destination _____

Date of Travel _____

Signature_____

Time to Pack!

Now that you're going to be living the life of a cowboy, you had better start to look like one. Your city-slicker clothes will never stand up to the rough and tough life of a cowboy. You need durable clothes.

As you pack you will need to include the following:

- jeans (at least 3 pairs)
- cowboy boots
- cowboy hat
- bandannas (at least one-half dozen, they are mighty useful on the ranch)
- long-sleeved cotton shirts (3)
- flannel shirts (2)

- long underwear (3 sets)
- socks (6 pairs)
- rain poncho
- belt
- bolo tie, fancy vest, and other luxury items (can be purchased if you can fit them into your budget)

Take a look at some catalogs like L.L. Bean, J.C. Penney, Eddie Bauer, Shepler's Western Wear, and Cheyenne Outfitters. Shop for and price the items you will need. Your trail boss has given you an $800.00 budget along with the order form below. Complete the form and show all of your work (on another sheet of paper, if necessary). When finished, return your order to your trail boss. The sooner you get your order in to the trail boss, the sooner you'll start looking like a cowboy instead of a greenhorn!

Catalog Name	Page No.	Item No.	Description	Color	Size	Qty.	Price Each	Total

Total _____

Morning Starters

1 Using the letters from the words dude ranch, how many other words can you make?

2 List ten vocabulary words that are associated with a dude ranch and then trade with someone and write the definitions to their words.

3 The answer is lariat. Make up three questions to go with that answer.

4 If you could ask Levi Strauss three questions, what would they be?

5 Write a letter to a relative back home describing an average day at the ranch.

6 List ten uses for a cowboy's hat.

7 List ten uses for a bandanna.

8 Make a list of the different types of geographic features you might see out West and draw them.

9 Write directions on how to saddle a horse for someone who has never done it before.

10 Make up a ghost story or tall tale that you could tell around a campfire.

11 List all of the types of cowboy clothing you can think of and their functions.

12 Use a map to follow one of the major cattle trails. Name the states through which it passes.

13 Create a brand using your initials, the initials of your school, or of your town.

14 Name five things that a cowboy carried on his horse and include their uses.

15 List the possible smells of a ranch and where they might come from.

16 ABC. . . Write a word that describes life on the ranch for each letter of the alphabet.

17 List the top ten reasons you would or would not like to be a cowboy/cowgirl.

18 What would you name a horse? Make a list of names, using words or phrases that describe the horse.

19 Make up a list of Western songs (real or fictional).

20 Design a birthday cake for a person on a ranch.

21 List a cowboy's top ten favorite birthday presents.

22 Describe what a horse's dream would be like.

23 In ___ minutes write all of the colors that you could imagine seeing on a ranch and where you would see them.

24 Write a short dialogue between two guests visiting a dude ranch.

25 Design a stationery letterhead and envelope for a dude ranch.

Cowboy Coupons

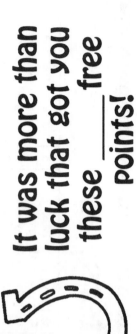

Your Brand of Work Is
A-OK.
Congratulations!
You have earned
_____

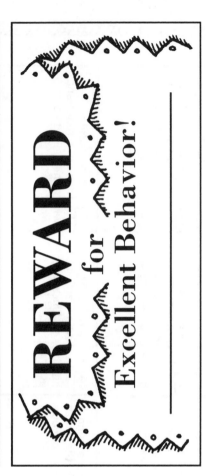

REWARD for
Excellent Behavior!
_____

It was more than
luck that got you
these _____ free
points!

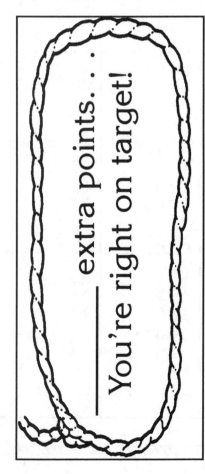

_____ extra points. . .
You're right on target!

FIRST RATE!
_____
_____
_____

Super!

HEAD 'EM OFF AT THE
PASS.
NO HOMEWORK!

Answer Key

Page 8

Page 9

Pages 10 and 11

1. vaqueros
2. chaparral
3. maverick
4. sombrero
5. Sacajawea
6. Conestoga
7. Chinese
8. Native Americans
9. lariat
10. buckaroos

Page 15

Clues:

1. Spurs
2. chaps
3. sombrero
4. gloves
5. branding
6. bandanna
7. cuffs
8. heel
9. tourniquet
10. John B.
11. mule-ears
12. hazing
13. herd
14. stitching

J	I	E	L	M	B	H	G	N	I	H	C	T	I	T	S
R	J	O	H	N	B	P	S	S	E	I	N	W	S	T	A
K	I	T	H	C	B	W	E	D	R	E	H	W	R	I	T
T	E	U	Q	I	N	R	U	O	T	U	M	Y	T	H	A
T	A	N	N	A	D	N	A	B	L	F	P	B	R	I	S
Q	S	E	A	L	M	U	L	E	E	A	R	S	I	E	F
G	P	R	E	W	A	N	S	I	T	J	M	I	V	A	F
B	A	E	N	R	S	O	M	B	R	E	R	O	L	O	U
F	H	J	K	O	K	W	I	J	V	M	L	L	R	N	C
Q	C	B	B	R	A	N	D	I	N	G	N	I	Z	A	H
K	D	J	E	M	L	O	K	S	D	P	E	K	V	O	E

Page 19

Teacher Note: If using the metric system, convert the measurements as needed to complete the activity.

1. 92 days
2.
flour	500	pounds
coffee beans	100	pounds
oatmeal	60	pounds
bacon	250	pounds
apples	100	pounds
lard	175	pounds
salt	150	pounds
corn starch	20	pounds
baking powder	16	pounds
rice	50	pounds
mustard	40	pounds
peppercorns	18	pounds
vinegar	30	pounds
sugar	250	pounds
tea	10	pounds
cornmeal	80	pounds
beans	100	pounds
prunes	15	pounds
raisins	25	pounds
allspice	3	pounds
baking soda	30	pounds
tomatoes	360	pounds
pickles	75	pounds
cinnamon	10	pounds
pancake syrup	40	pounds
3. Total=2507 pounds of supplies
4. 1253.5 pounds pulled by each horse
5. Answers will vary with each student.

Bonus: 50.14 pounds of food for each cowboy

Answer Key *(cont.)*

Page 21

Possible solution:

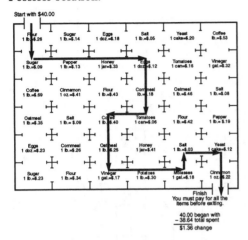

Page 26

Page 27

1. kinfolk
2. pioneer
3. Texas
4. California
5. ranch
6. homesite
7. prairie dog
8. coyote
9. critter
10. Horsefeathers
11. mountains
12. rattlesnake
13. varmint
14. round up
15. longhorn
16. hullaballoo
17. rodeo
18. stallion
19. Grand Canyon
20. Lightning
21. Pinnacle Pete
22. Slewfoot Sue
23. homesteader
24. descendants

Page 31

1. Sirius
2. Betelgeuse
3. Ursa Major
4. Orion
5. Andromeda
6. Cassiopeia
7. Rigel
8. Pegasus
9. Polaris

Pages 32-33

1. 7718—Bill
2. 808—Bob
3. 537—Les
4. 31770—Ollie
5. 0.981—1860
6. .05—So
7. 5538—Bess
8. 317537—Leslie
9. 312217—Lizzie
10. 5604—hogs
11. 35336—geese
12. 5538—Bess
13. 7738—Bell
14. 317537—Leslie
15. 77345—Shell
16. 312217—Lizzie
17. 663—egg
18. 607—Log
19. 7714—hill
20. 5508—Boss

Page 34

1. F
2. T
3. S
4. H
5. C
6. K
7. N
8. M
9. B
10. P
11. A
12. J
13. O
14. D
15. L
16. F
17. I
18. R
19. Q
20. G

Page 41

1. 10. Be sure to count the largest brand that divides the test into four parts.
2. Roosters don't lay eggs!
3. A one-story house has no stairs and therefore they can't be painted blue.
4. Pine trees have needles, not leaves.
5. You should have drawn a circle around the entire test, including the title, graphic, and questions.

Page 42

1	2	3
S	O	M
8	9	4
O	PICTURE	B
7	6	5
R	E	R

Box 4—boots
Box 7—rodeo
Box 1—saddle
Box 5—ranch
Box 2—outlaw
Box 8—owl
Box 3—Mexico
Box 6—ears

Answer Key (cont.)

Page 43

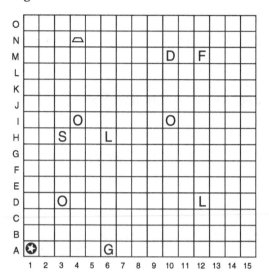

Answer: Fool's Gold

Page 44

House Color	Red	Yellow	Green	Blue	Brown
Ranch Hand	Vaquero	Buckaroo	Maverick	Cowpoke	Cowgirl
Pet	Armadillo	Coyote	Prairie Dog	Road Runner	Rattlesnake
Food	Trail Mix	Beef Stew	Baked Beans	Beef Jerky	Sourdough
Horse	Palomino	Dapple Gray	Black Stallion	Appaloosa	White Stallion

1. Vaquero
2. Cowgirl
3. Maverick
4. Buckaroo
5. Cowpoke

Page 46

1. dough
2. coarse
3. crusty
4. blend
5. flat
6. sour
7. beaten
8. Rising
9. seasoned
10. half-baked
11. sifted

	4000'-5000'	6000'-7000'	10,000'
shortening	1 cup	1 cup	1 cup
sugar	1½ cups	1½ cups	1½ cups
baking powder	5 tsp.	4 tsp.	3 tsp.
eggs	4 eggs	4 eggs	4 eggs
flour	8½ cups	9 cups	10 cups
vanilla	2 tsp.	2 tsp.	2 tsp.
milk	2 cups & 2 T	2 cups & 4 T	2 cups & 6 T

Teacher Note: If using the metric system, convert the measurements as needed to complete the activity.

Page 48
Picture: Cowboy hat

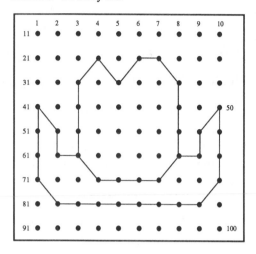

Page 55
1. "Everything is funny as long as it is happening to somebody else."
   *Bonus: 56 years old
2. "Home on the Range"

Page 57

1. E	5. C	9. N	13. N
2. N	6. U	10. R	14. N
3. D	7. I	11. D	
4. A	8. L	12. H	

Riddle answer: lunch and dinner

Page 59

1790, 1803, 1804, 1805, 1846, 1848, 1848, 1849, 1850, 1853, 1859, 1859, 1860, 1861, 1862, 1864, 1867, 1869, 1869, 1872, 1876, 1876, 1883, 1889, 1889, 1890, 1890, 1896, 1898

Page 60

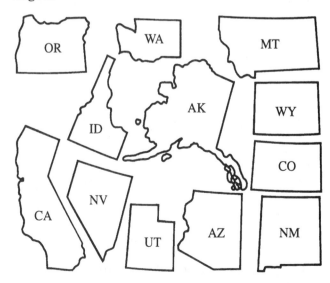

Bibliography

Axelrod, Alan and Dan Fox. *Songs of the Wild West.* Simon and Schuster, 1991.

Aylesworth, Virginia and Thomas. *Let's Discover the States: The Southwest.* Chelsea House, 1988.

Bellville, Cheryl Walsh. *Rodeo.* Carolrhoda Books, 1985.

Courtault, Martine. *Going West: Cowboys and Pioneers.* Young Discovery Library, 1989.

Delano, Sharon and David Rieff. *Texas Boots.* Viking Press, 1981.

Fenner, Phyllis. *Cowboys, Cowboys, Cowboys: Stories of Roundups and Rodeos, Branding and Broncobusting.* Franklin Watts, Inc., 1950.

Fisher, Evert. *The Oregon Trail.* Holiday House, 1990.

Folsom, Franklin. *Black Cowboy: The Life and Legend of George McJunkin.* Robert Rinehart Publishers, 1992.

Freedman, Russell. *Children of the Wild West.* Ticknor and Fields, 1983.

Freedman, Russell. *Cowboys of the Wild West.* Houghton Mifflin, 1985.

Greene, Carla. *Cowboys, What Do They Do?* Harper Row, 1972.

Hyde, Wayne. *What Does a Cowboy Do?* Dodd, Mead, and Company, 1963.

Katz, William Loren. *The Black West: A Documentary and Pictorial History.* Doubleday and Company, 1971.

Keating, Bern. *Famous American Cowboys.* Rand McNally and Company, 1977.

Kellog, Steven. *Pecos Bill.* William Morrow and Company, Inc., 1986.

Lightfoot, D.J. *Trail Fever: The Life of a Texas Cowboy.* Lothrop, 1992.

Lomax, John A. *Cowboy Songs and Other Frontier Ballads.* MacMillan Company, 1955.

Lyman, Nanci A. *Pecos Bill.* Troll Associates, 1980.

Martini, Terri. *Cowboys: A New True Book.* Childrens Press, 1987.

McCarthy, Bobbett (Illustrator). *Buffalo Girls.* Illus. Crown, 1987.

McDowell, Bart. *The American Cowboy in Life and Legend.* National Geographic Society, 1972.

Miller, Robert H. *Cowboys.* Silver Burdett, 1991.

Murdoch, David H. *Cowboy Eyewitness Book.* Alfred A. Knopf, Inc., 1993.

Pelz, Ruth. *Black Heroes of the Wild West.* Open Hand Publishing, Inc. 1990.

Roach, Joyce Gibson. *The Cowgirls.* University of North Texas Press, 1990.

Rounds, Glen. *Cowboys.* Holiday House, 1991.

Slatta, Richard W. *Cowboys of the Americas.* Yale University Press, 1990.

Steber, Rick. *Cowboys.* Bonanza Publishing, 1988.